Cambridge Studies in Social Anthropology

General Editor: Jack Goody

14

SPIRITS OF PROTEST

OTHER TITLES IN THE SERIES

Spirits of Protest

Spirit-mediums and the articulation
of consensus among the Zezuru of
Southern Rhodesia (Zimbabwe)

PETER FRY
Lecturer in Anthropology
Universidade Estadual de Campinas, Brazil

Cambridge University Press

Cambridge
London   New York   Melbourne

Published by the Syndics of the Cambridge University Press
The Pitt Building, Trumpington Street, Cambridge CB2 1RP
Bentley House, 200 Euston Road, London NW1 2DB
32 East 57th Street, New York, NY 10022, USA
296 Beaconsfield Parade, Middle Park, Melbourne 3206, Australia

First published 1976

Printed in Great Britain
at the University Printing House, Cambridge
(Euan Phillips, University Printer)

Library of Congress Cataloguing in Publication Data
Fry, Peter.
    Spirits of protest.
    (Cambridge studies in social anthropology; 14)
    Bibliography: p.
    Includes index.
    1. Zezuru (Bantu people) – Religion.
2. Spiritualism – Zimbabwe African People's Union.
I. Title.
BL2480.Z4F79   299'.6   75-20832
ISBN 0 521 21052 6

Contents

Acknowledgments

The research on which this book is based was financed by a Commonwealth Scholarship for which I thank the Federal Commonwealth Board.

During my research I was fortunate in being affiliated to the Department of Sociology at the University College of Rhodesia and Nyasaland (now the University College of Rhodesia). There I was given much valuable encouragement and assistance through Professor Clyde Mitchell's Research Seminar. Latterly Professor Jaap van Velsen has provided thoughtful criticism and advice and I have had persistent help and encouragement from the Department of Anthropology at University College London, in particular from the late Professor Daryll Forde and my research supervisor, Professor Mary Douglas.

To the Universidade Estadual de Campinas in Brazil I am grateful for a sabbatical three months, to Dr Rupert Sheldrake, Dr Keith, Jean and Alison Campbell and Mr Carlos da Silva for providing the conditions necessary for writing, to Mr David Trevitchik for genealogies and diagrams and to Mrs G. Halstead, Mrs P. Blair and Mrs A. Warwick for their typing. I thank Mr S.W. Averiett for support in trying times.

The debt which cannot ever be settled is with the people of Chiota and all the many Africans who gave me the privelege of sharing their life over two and a half years. It would be invidious to mention names for my friends and helpers were many. To all of them I express my deepest thanks and gratitude.

Conventions

I shall adopt the convention of putting all spirit names in italic; one proper name followed by another in italic refers to a medium in trance. Thus David/*Kafudzi* means David possessed by *Kafudzi*. The people of Chiota did not always make it clear whether they were referring to a spirit *qua* spirit, to a spirit presented through a medium or to a spirit-medium who was not in trance. Thus in everyday speech, 'Kafudzi' could mean either *Kafudzi* acting independently of its present medium, *Kafudzi* as presented by David in trance, or David as a normal person. The convention that I have adopted makes it possible to make these distinctions while retaining the 'confusions'.

After the research on which this book is based, Rhodesian currency was decimalised. I have, however, retained the old notation of pounds, shillings and pence.

Names of individuals and certain spirits have been altered, and at times I have merged two people into one and vice versa.

Introduction

The fieldwork situation

Southern Rhodesia in the first half of the 1960s was the scene of many confrontations. African nationalism which had got under way towards the end of the 1950s had been met with a strong white nationalism which swept the polls with the election to power of Mr Smith's Rhodesia Front party. In 1963 the African Nationalist movement split into two bitterly opposed parties, the People's Caretaker Council (PCC) and the Zimbabwe African National Union (ZANU) who fought with one another for the right to represent the mass of the people. During my fieldwork in Chiota Tribal Trust Land, ZANU and the PCC were banned, Mr Smith declared unilaterial independence from Britain, and the world reacted with economic sanctions against Rhodesia. African leaders were rounded up and put either in detention or in restriction in camps miles out in the bush and the situation returned to an uneasy peace maintained by a constantly renewed State of Emergency under which the minority white government used its extra-ordinary powers to thwart any kind of overt opposition on the part of the Africans.

The task of the fieldworker, which is not easy in any situation, was therefore daunting. Anthropologists fall into none of 'the known and accepted categories, neither missionary nor preacher, trader nor administrator' (van Velsen 1964 : xix) and there was plenty of scope for both the people of Chiota and the government to imagine what my purposes could be. To begin work in Chiota required the permission of the District Commissioner in Marandellas and of the African council which met in Mahusekwa, the central township of the area. The meeting was turbulent. While the chiefs present supported my application (three of them offered houses in which to stay), a number of the elected councillors[1] raised serious objections. Had not Cecil Rhodes claimed to be a friend; had he not given rise to the situation which now prevailed where Africans were being dominated by the whites and denied their true worth as citizens?

However, the council finally agreed to my working in the area (they could hardly refuse, for I was, after all, white) and I took up residence in the village of one of the chiefs, where I spent the first three months.

For the first year the position was difficult. Many of the people of Chiota thought that I was an emissary of the government and during the period of strife between ZANU and the PCC I was even accused by each of being a member of the other. As often as I tried to deny any allegiance to the police or government

1

I was faced with evidence to the contrary. The Special Branch of the British South Africa Police visited me in their Land Rover to ask about my political affiliations, my views on African nationalism and my strange tastes for African beer, African food, and African friends. The suspicions of the 'Europeans' continued, and although the people of Chiota became more and more friendly, they could never come to terms with what I was really trying to do. Most people believed that my living there was a hardship (on the contrary I enjoyed it) and that there must therefore be a pay-off in the end. Others continued to believe that I was inextricably linked with the government.

They were, of course, quite right; even if I disagreed with the policies of Mr Smith's government, and even if I felt that I was being unjustly identified with them, I was white, and had benefited from the accident of birth which made me English. I did not have to endure that kind of life for ever; as a white man I could be assured of a certain respect from the police; and, in the last analysis, I would be able to earn my living as an anthropologist on the basis of the information which the people of Chiota could give me. As long as social anthropology continues to study the underdogs this will always be the case.

With all these difficulties I had to work as unobtrusively as possible, and the material on which this book is based was gathered more from the passive observation of social and ritual life than from the asking of questions in formal interview situations. I realise that a certain amount of statistical information would have been of great value, especially in relation to the social characteristics of spirit-mediums, but when I once launched a very simple survey of a small number of villages the reaction threatened to prejudice whatever goodwill I had succeeded in establishing.

The pace of fieldwork, then, was dictated by circumstance, rather than design, and I had to make the best advantage of anything that came my way. Although these tactics meant that I was unable to collect material systematically, they had the enormous advantage of allowing me to keep a relatively open mind and to be sensitive to matters of importance which might otherwise have escaped my notice. Indeed, it was by chance that my attention came finally to be focused on spirit-mediumship and religion.

The emergence of a problem

Chiota Tribal Trust Land had originally been chosen for research because of its proximity to Salisbury. It was known that many of the able-bodied men of Chiota worked in the town during the week and returned to their villages, where they left their wives and children, at weekends, and it was hoped to make a study of this kind of labour migration with fieldwork both in the countryside and in the town.

Due to the tense political situation this was perhaps the most difficult aspect of social life that I could have chosen to study; not only was it impossible to work freely in the African townships which were under heavy police control, but it was also very difficult to probe into such details as family budgets, job experience and the like for the simple reason that such questions were usually only asked by policemen. The systematic collection of information relating to life histories, kinship and friendship was therefore well nigh impossible.

From the start of my fieldwork I had intended not to be preoccupied with studying religion and ritual, mainly because of my interest in making a contribution to an understanding of what were considered to be more basic matters, but also because I had been led to believe that 'traditional' beliefs and practices were dying out and were of little significance to the contemporary situation.[2]

However, bit by bit I became aware of the fact that this was by no means the case. Rituals were a regular weekend occurrence in many villages, the number of persons who were succumbing to spirit-mediumship was increasing, churches were being burned and stoned and these events were the subject of much comment and speculation. It became quite clear that 'traditional' beliefs and practices were related to the rise of African nationalism and as such of considerable relevance to the social life of the people of Chiota.

At first my attempts to attend seances were frustrated, and I was generally politely turned away from them with the explanation that the spirits present were of people who had lived and died before the arrival of the whites in Southern Rhodesia; they would not, therefore, like to have a white person presented to them. When I discovered that one prominent medium had been visited by the police and had been found in possession of PCC party cards it became clear that I had chosen an even more sensitive area of social life and resigned myself to even greater frustration.

However, when my assistant himself started to develop the symptoms of spirit-mediumship I began to gain easier access to other mediums and when, quite by chance, I gave a lift to one of the most popular mediums of Chiota, my luck turned. He expressed his thanks and offered me unlimited access to his seances. The support which he gave me meant that other mediums who had previously been hostile opened their doors and I was able to spend about three months living at this medium's village as a honorary member of his administrative staff. I made myself useful where I could; my car was used for visits to outlying village rituals; I used what small influence I had as a white man to facilitate certain negotiations and I learned to play the thumb-piano (*mbira*) which meant that I could occupy a place with the musicians in the seance house (*banya*). The hospitality that I received was so great as to be embarrassing. The guilt that I felt as a member of the dominant colour group in Rhodesia which denies the majority of black people the status of social equals became even more poignant.

The data on which this book is based were collected, then, by the observation of events at this medium's village, from visits to other important mediums and from events which I observed in the three villages where I stayed, one in the chieftaincy of Chief Chiota and two in the chieftaincy of Chief Nenguo.

3

The first chapter sets the social and economic background, the second the fundamental aspects of Zezuru magico-religious beliefs. In chapter 3 I discuss spirit-mediums and the nature of their authority, arguing that this is based on the ability of spirit-mediums to express and articulate common consensus. In chapter 4 I compare the charismatic flexibility of religious organisation in Chiota with the more rigidly organised Korekore system and in chapter 5 I present and analyse an extended case which concerns the entry into spirit-mediumship of my field assistant and the effects of this both in relation to the politics of 'low-level' mediums of ancestor spirits in his village and to the power politics of what I have called 'high-level' mediums who are believed to be possessed by powerful hero spirits and whose scale of operations extends beyond the boundaries of kin group, village or chiefdom. The final chapter is devoted to an account of the decline of Christianity in Chiota and the rise of spirit-mediumship in the context of the confrontation between black and white nationalism in Southern Rhodesia.

The emphasis of the analysis is on the flexibility of Zezuru beliefs and of Zezuru religious organisation. Spirit-mediums are not portrayed as actors of social roles arranged in a neat and stable hierarchy that has been hallowed by tradition, but as essentially charismatic figures whose creative energy in sensing public opinion, forming and moulding it into support and occasionally collective political action has a continuous effect on the relations of spirit-mediums to one another and to the lay public. Religious figures do not control the use of physical sanctions to enforce their decisions, they can only maintain their authority if their claims to sacredness are believed in, although the people of Chiota are committed to a belief in the inevitable powers of *particular* spirit-mediums or of the spirits which they claim to represent. Spirits, in the last analysis, are the creation of society; they come into being, rise and fall from grace through the energies of their mediums who attempt to satisfy the religious aspirations of the people whom they serve and to fulfil their own vocations as prophets, diviners and healers.

I

The secular background

Spirit-mediums play many roles but in the main they are concerned with the analysis of extra-ordinary situations, especially ill-health and other misfortunes. The theory on which they draw to make their analyses attempts to explain misfortune in terms of mystical forces set in motion as a result of social disturbance.

As will be shown later in this study, spirit-mediums operate at various levels of social structure, but broadly speaking they can be distinguished as 'high-level' mediums and 'low-level' mediums. The latter operate at village level and deal with purely local problems, while the former deal with affairs which surpass purely village and lineage interests. However, even village problems are often affected by events which occur outside village limits, and spirit mediums in general have to analyse the extra-ordinary in terms not only of the social structure of Chiota, but of the wider structure of Rhodesia, itself involved in British and world affairs.

Before turning specifically to spirit-mediumship, therefore, it is essential to examine the basic secular characteristics of social life.

Chiota is denominated a 'Tribal Trust Land' and it is supposed that there reigns a 'tribal order'. However, this 'tribal' order does not exist simply as a manifestation of the inertia of 'tradition',[1] but also as a consequence of diverse political and economic forces. Chiota is not an island. On the contrary, it is very much involved in the wider polity of Rhodesia and the world outside, for its sheer proximity to Salisbury has drawn its people out of the narrow interests of village, kin group and chiefdom, into the economic interests generated by the capitalist structure of the national economy and the political interests generated by the colonial situation. It is not an exaggeration to say that the Prime Minister of England, and the British American Tobacco Corporation (BAT) enter into the consciousness of the people of Chiota as much as their chiefs and headmen.

It is the concern of this chapter briefly to lay down the fundamental socio-economic background out of which are produced the problems which the spirit-mediums analyse.

The political and administrative framework

Rhodesia is governed from the capital, Salisbury, by a legislature elected by those who qualify for the franchise. In effect most voters are white, as is at least 75% of the membership of the legislature.

5

The land is divided up into African and European areas, whereby whites and blacks are separated residentially. Of the African areas, 8,052,000 acres are set aside for 'Native Purchase Areas' where Africans may buy small farms, and there are 33,898,000 acres of Tribal Trust Land, where Africans live according to 'tribal' patterns.

Chiota is one such Tribal Trust Land situated some 45 miles south-east of Salisbury and 25 miles west of Marandellas. The area is dominated by tobacco cultivation on large European-owned farms which border Chiota on two sides. On the other boundaries are the Native Purchase Areas of Muda to the west and Chimbandwa to the south.

The region in which Chiota is situated is traditionally the home of the Zezuru, a subgroup of the Shona speaking congeries who are also to be found in other Tribal Trust Lands in Central Rhodesia, such as Zvimba, Chiweshe, Chinamora, Chikwakwa, Seke, Goromonzi, Mhondoro, Wedza, Soswe and Mrewa. The Zezuru differ in minor structural and cultural ways from the three other major Shona speaking groups, the Korekore in the north-east, the Karanga in the south and the Manyika in the east.[2]

The Tribal Trust Lands are administered through the Ministry of Internal Affairs according to what the government recognises as 'tribal institutions'. For these purposes the country is divided up into provinces and districts and Chiota falls in the District of Marandellas, which town is the headquarters of the District Commissioner (DC).

Contact between Africans and the DCs is through the 'tribal leaders', the chiefs and headmen. These offices represent the apex of the 'tribal' hierarchy and the lowest echelons of the administrative hierarchy of the colony. They are responsible to the DCs for collecting personal tax (£2 per year) and for the dissemination of government edicts and information. Chiefs are still responsible for the apportionment of land within the reserves, but their powers are largely circumscribed by the terms of the Land Husbandry Act of 1955, by which the land holdings of individuals and the head of cattle each individual may own are geared to the amount of arable land and grazing land available in each reserve.[3] The judicial system also makes use of tribal institutions. Cases which are not settled at village level pass up to ward level and then to the chief. Appeal may then be made from the chief's court to the district magistrate. Criminal cases can not be dealt with in chiefs' courts.

In Chiota there is also an African council, with offices in the central township of Mahusekwa. The DC is *ex officio*, president of the council and the five chiefs, Chiota, Nenguo, Nyandoro, Mudzimerema and Samuriwo are *ex officio* vice-presidents with voting power. The other members of the council consist of the four ward headmen (*machinda*) and then fifteen elected councillors, four from the Chiota area, four from Nenguo, three from Nyandoro and two each from Samuriwo and Mudzimerema.

Apart from funds occasionally provided by the government to aid certain

6

projects, the income of the Council is from rates which are collected annually, 5s per plot holder, and from cattle dipping fees which are 2s 6d or 2s per beast per year. In addition money comes in from the sale of timber and dog licences. This money is used to employ a full-time secretary and messenger, and the people who run the cattle dipping tanks and a primary school. The African councils are being encouraged to take over the running of community affairs as part of a general policy on the part of the government to establish 'community development' in Rhodesia. The powers of councils as laid down in the African Council's Act (1957) are that they may do 'any act or thing specified in the warrant which in the opinion of the Minister should or could be done by such council for the welfare, advantage and betterment of the community of inhabitants of the area'.

The council, like the DC, makes extensive use of the tribal hierarchy for executing much of its business, such as the policing of timber plantations, the collection of rates and dip fees, and the dissemination of information.

Three levels of organisation are recognised by the government, which correspond to 'traditional' political forms. They are the village (*musha*), the ward (*dunhu*, pl. *matunhu*) and the chiefdom (*nyika*). This basic pattern has been well described by Holleman (1949, 1952).

The village

Present day villages are built in lines (*maraini*) along surveyed contours separating the higher lying arable land from the lower lying grazing land. In general they consist of four parallel lines formed by the granaries (nearest the arable land), bedrooms, kitchens and then at a distance of about 100 yards, the cattle kraals. They vary in size from 10 to 100 nuclear families each with their own kitchens and granaries which are clustered into village sections (*mana*), defined by their leaders (*samana*). The size, that is the number of nuclear families, and composition of the *mana* depends on the stage reached in their development cycle, but does not usually exceed a man, his wives, his married sons and their wives and children (marriage is virilocal), his unmarried sons and unmarried, divorced or widowed daughters, and perhaps their children, and maybe a sister. Although each nuclear family preserves a considerable amount of economic independence, members of the same *mana* do help each other in the fields and by exchanging food and small services. They are also tied together with common interest in bridewealth earned by its women and used by its men to marry in their turn.

Each village is based on a patrilineage core, to which other village members besides wives are related either cognatically or affinally; there are sometimes strangers (*vatorwa*). From this patrilineage is selected the village headman. He holds a court (*dare*) at which local disputes are first tried, and from which appeal is to the court of the subchief or chief. He also holds the lowest office of the administrative hierarchy and is responsible for conveying important messages from the chief to his people. Furthermore, he is responsible for collecting the

7

personal tax of the people on his book. (Village headmen are most often called 'sabuku', literally the owner of the book, as members of his village are entered in a book which has become the symbol of his office). The village headman also is the first person to be approached should a member of his 'book' require land to plough. His support is valuable in dealings with the chief, whose decision is final in this matter.

Institutionalised co-operation at village level is minimal and in such activities as ploughing and harvesting, co-operation beyond the level of the *mana* is based on ties of friendship and kinship, or is purely contractual (e.g. the exchange of beer for labour at beer parties).

Holleman (1952 : 12) described the ward as primarily a territorial unit with rights in land. However, under the terms of the African Land Husbandry Act (1951) this is no longer the case as each village has its own block of land, tenure of which is regulated directly by the chief.

The chiefdom

The chiefdom is the largest tribal unit, and the chief (*ishe*) is selected from the lineage core of the chiefdom. After Garbett (1963a) I shall refer to such lineages as 'royal lineages'. Succession disputes are common, and result from the rather vague succession rules based on a combination of adelphic and rotational principles. Interregna may last for upwards of three years, and although the choice of successor lies ostensibly with members of the chiefdom, the new chief must be ratified in his office by the DC. He is then paid a salary by the government.

The chief's duties, therefore, are those of a multipurpose civil servant. He holds the highest court (*dare*) in his chiefdom, appeal from which is to the district magistrate (in the case of Chiota this is to the magistrate in Marandellas). He is responsible for the collection of personal tax and council rates and dip fees. He is also responsible for the allocation of land under the terms of the Land Husbandry Act, although appeal may be made to the DC through the Agricultural Officer and the chief must inform the DC of all allocations.

Shona chiefs, then, occupy the familiar 'intercalary' role, analysed by Mitchell (1956) and Gluckman *et al.* (1949), for, while being the representatives of their people to the government, they are also the representatives of the government to the people. They are as much government servants as tribal leaders.[4]

The 'tribal structure' of Chiota, then, with its chiefs, subchiefs and village headman, although seen by people and government as representing the continuity of 'traditional' pre-colonial structures, persists in its present form largely because of government policy and action whence it derives its apparent stability. The 'tribal' order is convenient for government administration as has been shown above, and is also convenient in political terms, as became very clear in October 1964 when, as part of its strategy to bargain independence from Britain, the Rhodesian government called together all chiefs and headmen (subchiefs) to the

8

The secular background

'Domboshawa Indaba' in order to find out African opinion on the independence issue. In the White Paper published after the Indaba, the government justified this method of testing African opinion by analysing the 'tribal structure' as if government played no part whatsoever in its functioning. Chiefs were represented as consensual leaders of their people and thus able to speak for them.

In fact, the chiefs depend for their positions, income and prestige on government support, and in the isolation of the 'Domboshawa Indaba', after an impressive display of Rhodesian armed might, they committed their people to support the Rhodesian Prime Minister in his policy of independence from Britain under a white minority government.

The people of Chiota were not surprised by this unanimous decision of the chiefs, for they are well aware of the dependence of their chiefs on government goodwill. However, they did not agree with the chiefs' decision and, significantly, it was a spirit-medium who affirmed that had government called together the spirit-mediums rather than the chiefs, the result would have been radically different. Later in this study the coercive authority of chiefs will be contrasted with the consensual authority of spirit-mediums.

The Economic Background

Just as the 'tribal structure' of Chiota is fully incorporated into the administrative and political structure of Rhodesia as a whole, so is the economic system. The people of Chiota not only cultivate such crops as maize, millet and groundnuts, and tend cattle for their subsistence, they also sell their surplus on the open market. Furthermore, the relative infertility of the soil and the proximity of Chiota to Salisbury force working men to sell their labour in the industry and commerce of the capital, and also to a lesser extent on the white-owned farms which border Chiota.[5]

On Friday evenings in Chiota plumes of smoke rise over many villages as women complete the final process in the brewing of beer, in preparation for the anticipated arrival of the menfolk who work in Salisbury and who fill the many buses which travel the forty-five miles of well maintained road between Salisbury and Chiota. The weekends are a time of social regeneration and recreation after the workaday week of women in the fields and men in town. Beer is drunk in large quantities either for ritual purposes (rituals are held at weekends so that the men may be present) or for cash, when the women of Chiota exchange their crops for the wages of the working men.

Most Chiota men, as they reach working age, leave for the towns, particularly Salisbury, but continue to maintain close links with Chiota, returning home most weekends. This situation is made possible by Chiota's proximity to Salisbury and the frequency of buses. The return fare is 9s. In addition, those who own cars ply backwards and forwards carrying passengers who are charged the standard bus fare.

Spirits of protest

The basic pattern, then, is that men spend their weekdays in town, so long as they have a job. When they lose their jobs either through old age, redundancy, or sickness, they return to their villages.

The figures of the 1962 African census give a clear indication of the rate of labour migration in Chiota. The census was taken during the week, and thus represents the population of Chiota with many of the working men away. Doubtless had the census been taken on a Saturday evening, the number of men would have been greater.

Date of Birth	−1918	1918−1945	1945−	Total
Males	1,230	2,240	7,330	10,800
Females	1,550	4,840	7,060	13,450
Both	2,780	7,080	14,390	24,250

It will be noticed that the greatest disparity between the sexes is the age group 17–44 where there are approximately twice as many women as men present in the reserve. Although they may not all be away working, it is nevertheless reasonable to assume a rate of 50%; persons away visiting kin will be compensated for by other kin visiting in Chiota who will of course be included in the figures.

Undoubtedly the dominant factor in maintaining this pattern of commuter labour is economic. Although other factors, such as inter-personal relations, the desire to see the 'bright lights' (Gulliver 1957 : 58), may affect the *incidence* of labour migration, they do not affect the *rate*.

Furthermore, as Mitchell (1959) has pointed out, 'an analysis of labour migration . . . must set out to explain not only why the men leave their tribal home, and the causes for this may be more complicated than merely economic reasons — but also why they should constantly circulate between their tribal homes and the labour centres'. Thus, in the Chiota situation, it is important to consider not only those factors which 'push' men out of the reserve into the town ('centrifugal' pressures), but also those which 'pull' them back again ('centripetal' pressures).

Chiota men are forced into the town for economic reasons and, in order to achieve social and economic security, they are in turn forced to maintain links with the countryside so that they may return there in the event of their being no longer able to work in town. The Chiota situation thus parallels that of other situations reported for Central Africa, notably the Lakeside Tonga (van Velsen 1961, 1964), the Mambwe (Watson 1958) and other situations in which labour migration results not in a breakdown of the rural society, but contributes to its maintenance, providing, in cash and goods, the wherewithal to sustain an ever-increasing population (the 1962 African Census predicted that the African population of Rhodesia would double in twenty years) in a fixed area which is declining in fertility.

Largely because Chiota is perceived as an ultimate security against the vicis-

10

situdes of town life, the men of Chiota in general continue to participate in Chiota life although physically distant from it. This is of course facilitated by the good communications which exist between Chiota and Salisbury, but it is manifest also by the way in which Chiota people tend to live near to each other in the towns, spend their leisure time with other Chiota people and utilise their Chiota-based networks in job hunting, etc. Although, from the outsider's point of view, Chiota has been absorbed into the national economy, the people of Chiota have absorbed the town into their rural-based social fields. 'My fields are in the town' (*minda yanga iri kutowini*) was the way in which one worker expressed this idea. In this sense, the strategy of the majority of Chiota people resembles that of the Red Xhosa as reported by Mayer (1963), for although they work in the towns and *may* remain absent from Chiota for extended peiods, they remain 'encapsulated' in a Chiota-orientated network of social relations.

A further way in which working men maintain their interest in the rural society is by leaving behind their wives and children. The reasons for this strategy are both political and economic. By leaving their wives behind, the men can hope to maintain their interests in village affairs. But at the same time women are economically more efficient in the countryside than in the towns. Whereas women in town tend to be just one more mouth to feed in economic terms (although there are those who run the risk of brewing and selling beer illicitly, and the few who work, largely as domestic servants), women in the countryside make an important economic contribution. They cultivate the family fields, thus alleviating the cost of feeding their families, and also convert a portion of their harvests of millet and maize into beer which provides cash to buy small luxuries such as sugar, tea and bread, and to help buy clothing and pay for the education of their children.

Women have thus come to play a very important part in community and family affairs.[6] Chiota families have a distinctly matri-focal aspect and perhaps more than ever before women are able to make their position felt, as will be shown later in this chapter.

The general picture, then, is of a rural area producing a limited amount of agricultural produce, sustained in large part by the men who work in the city. Schools are built to educate the children left behind with their mothers, stores spring up in all corners to cater for the needs of those who stay behind, and the economic state of the area is a function more of the economic situation of the country as a whole than of its agricultural production alone. It is for this reason, perhaps, that spirit-mediums are as much concerned with the state of the labour market in Salisbury as they are with rain.

The economic and political innovations which have occurred since the arrival of Cecil Rhodes' British South Africa Company in 1890 have therefore affected drastically the social life of Chiota. But, as has been emphasised, the basic 'tribal' institutions have remained solid and many of the changes are 'thought of' in terms of old concepts. The most dramatic manifestation of this tendency is un-

11

doubtedly the way in which the cultural nationalism of the people of Chiota, a product of the dramatic political change of the fifties and sixties came to find its outlet in the cult of the spirit-mediums, but just as important, if less dramatic, is the continued relevance of kinship ideology in the structuring of social relationships.

Kinship

The Shona are divided into a number of dispersed patrilineal clans and subclans. The former are distinguished by 'totem' names (*mutupo*) such as *shumba* (lion) and *nzou* (elephant) and the latter by praise names (*chidawo*). Thus the members of Nenguo subclan possess the totem name Shumba and subclan praise name of Nyamuziva. Zezuru clans follow the common Central African pattern (Gluckman 1950) in being dispersed and exogamous, and fellow clan members are expected to treat one another as brothers and to succour one another in times of hardship.

When two strangers meet, they first exchange their respective praise names which establish an initially broad kinship relationship, which may subsequently be refined by exchange of further information about their particular lineages and the names of their fathers.

The largest lineages (*dzinza*) are those with interests in chiefly office (see above, p. 8). They are usually segmented into two or three major lineages (*imba*) about which the chiefship rotates. The corporateness of these chiefly lineages and their major segments rests in their common interest in chiefship, which is enshrined in the name (*zita*) of their founding ancestor. Segments of chiefly lineages only emerge as political units during succession crises.

The word *imba* (literally house) is a relative term and is made specific by reference to a particular ancestor. Thus, a member of the Nenguo lineage will say that he is of the Nenguo *dzinza*, but he is also of the *imba* of Chikukutu, and he may then further refine his lineage personality by referring to which matrisegment of his father's polygynous family he belongs.

The core lineages of wards (*matunhu*) similarly maintain a degree of corporateness because of their interest in a common office as to a lesser extent do the core lineages of villages (*misha*), but commoner lineages rarely exceed four generations in depth.

The significant kinship grouping is the patrilineal extended family inhabiting a *mana* (village section), for this group recognises the authority of a common 'father' (*baba*) who administers the common property. Such groups do not consist only of agnatic kin, there being affinally linked women and, occasionally, matrilaterally linked kin. Such kindreds are referred to by the term *mhuri* and are defined with reference to the person whose authority the groups recognise.

In this context Holleman's observations amongst the Hera, a further subgrouping of the Shona, are pertinent:

The secular background

The term *samhuri* (head of a *mhuri*) is sometimes used with reference to the head of a small village when its community consists of a group of near kindred who may be regarded as a single *mhuri*. It may also be used for a man in his capacity as head of his own family unit. But these references do not carry the specific political implications connected with *samusha* (village headman) or the geneaological rank and responsibility of a term like 'father' (*baba*). The position of the *samhuri* is a casual one, based on the esteem of a number of neighbouring multilineal kinsmen, and it lacks the formal and hereditary character of a position founded upon a unilineal structure. Except over his own family unit the authority of a *samhuri* is personal rather than legal. (Holleman 1952 : 29, 30)

When a patrilineage is vested with rights in chiefship, then it tends to attain considerable size and depth (up to nine generations). When such office is lacking, however, corporate descent groups are much smaller in span and depth. This fact is apparent from the rules of succession to property and office.

On dying, a man leaves behind him his office, symbolised by his name (*zita*) and his estate (*nhaka*). The successor to his name also assumes control of the estate, which is composed of his wives, ploughs and other property, his cattle and also the cattle which will accrue on the marriage of his unmarried daughters. In figure 1, A, B, C, D, E, F, G are personal names of males, b, c, d, e, f, g are the names of lineage females. a1, a3, b1, b2, c1, c2 are the names of lineage wives. Thus, D is a member of the *dzinza* of A, but he is also a member of B's *imba* with relation to F, and a member of the *imba* of b1, with relation to E.

On the death of A, B, his eldest son by his senior wife takes over the name (this is marked by A1). He thus succeeds to the position of his father and is called 'father' by the rest of the lineage. It is his duty to administer A's estate, receiving the bridewealth which comes in on the marriage of b and c and providing cattle for the marriage of his 'brothers' (e.g. C). On B's death, C succeeds to the name A, becoming A2. He continues to control the same estate, but he does not control the estate of B. This is done by D, who succeeds to the name B, becoming B1. It is his duty to administer the cattle coming in from the marriage of d and e and providing cattle for the marriage of E. On the death of C, the office of A reverts to the *imba* of a1, and is taken by D, who becomes A3. D now has the office of A, and B controlling the common estate of all the descendants of A and the common estate of the descendants of B. On his death, the title A passes back to the *imba* of a2 and is taken by its senior agnate, F. F is now the holder of the headship of the whole lineage founded by A, and also controls the estate of his father's segment. However, he does not succeed to B's name: this is inherited by E who becomes B2.

At this stage, the lineage will only persist as a corporate unit if it recognises the overall authority of F (A4) whether or not there is still any corporately owned property. If the name of A is of importance (e.g. chiefly or subchiefly office) then the lineage will continue to proliferate and the office will continue to rotate between the two *imba* defined with reference to a1 and a2. If, however,

13

Fig. 1

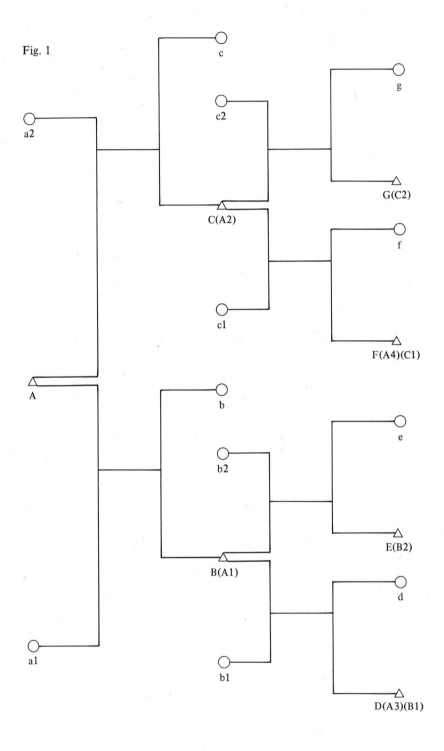

A does not carry with it any rank, then the lineage will split regularly, as the only basis for its continuance, i.e. the administration of a corporate estate, will disappear.

According to Zezuru ideals, all the sons of A are 'brothers' respecting one another according to their relative seniority. Again this should apply to the sons of B and C, who refer to B and C as fathers (*madzibaba*). There is a strong emphasis on the solidarity of lineages which, if put into practice, would result in enormous lineages, manifesting an idyllic social harmony where everyone fulfilled his full quota of kinship rights and duties.

In actual fact, the solidarity of lineages is prejudiced by individual self interest and the more cogent solidarity of matrisegments. I quote from Holleman:

There is on the one hand a natural cohesion between the various estate units based upon the solidarity of the various houses or a common patri-group and the right of control of the representative head of the latter group over the reproductive assets (cattle, wives, daughters) of the common estate. On the other hand, there is the recognition that the assets in each estate unit primarily belong to the particular house which has produced them, and consequently there is a tendency amongst the members of such an individual house to preserve these assets for their own benefit to the exclusion of other component houses of the common patri-group. In short, there is an inherent conflict between the principle of community of estate with its unified control, and the preferential claims or 'proprietary' rights of the different houses of the common patri-group. (Holleman 1952 : 325)

In pre-colonial times, it seems that such conflicts within lineages of various sizes were resolved in the last analysis by fission, with one group hiving off either to form the nucleus of a new community of which it would ultimately acquire the status of chiefship, or else to adhere to another already established chiefdom.

Nowadays, however, increasing population pressure on the land has made the resolution of such conflicts through fission rather more difficult so that kinship groups grow in size and tensions mount. Furthermore, changing economic conditions contribute to an increase in the incidence of tensions provenant from the clashes of individual and group interests.

Whereas, in the past, sons were dependent on their fathers for the cattle with which to marry and men depended on their kin for co-operation in their agricultural enterprises, nowadays the possibility of wage employment has emancipated the young from parental economic control and led to the possibility of individually earned fortunes. Conflict between lineage and individual interests has therefore been exacerbated and the old means of resolution have become inadequate.

An inherent feature of any patrilineal system which has been noted by Fortes, Evans-Pritchard and others is that women, as wives and mothers, operate as nodes of segmentation of the lineages into which they marry. There seems little doubt that Zezuru mothers were always a threat to lineage solidarity, simply because they generated strongly solidary matrisegments within the lineage of their husbands. But nowadays this tendency is surely the greater, as women acquire ever greater economic and political significance in lineage and village affairs.

Whether or not women really do contribute to antipathy between brothers, it is convenient to pin the blame for lineage disharmony on them as a means of avoiding open conflict between brothers. By putting the blame on their wives, brothers are able to deny (at least in public utterance) their own animosities against one another.

Cases of public and open dispute between lineage brothers are rare. In general such battles are fought either between their wives, or between the ancestors. Competition within lineages for economic or political control finds its expression in mutual accusations of witchcraft and sorcery and in the competition for favour with the ancestors, as interested groups attempt to assert their ritual supremacy through rival spirit-mediums. In subsequent chapters it will be shown how spirit-mediums act as foci of political and economic interest groups and how these groups challenge one another through the actions and utterances of mediums in trance.

Chiota in wider perspective

Throughout this chapter the emphasis has been placed on the close involvement of Chiota Tribal Trust Land with the wider polity, and on the importance of this fact for an understanding of social relations within the area. The sheer proximity of Chiota to Salisbury and the fact that most of the men of Chiota work for most of their lives in the factories, commerce and private homes of the dominant colour group means that Chiota society suffers the full impact of economic and political transformations on the national scene, which in its turn, is profoundly affected by British and international politics.

The people of Chiota were heavily committed to political action before the African Nationalist parties were banned by the Rhodesian government in 1964 and have indirectly suffered from the effects of the economic sanctions applied against Rhodesia by Britain and the United Nations Organisation in reprisal for the unilateral declaration of independence by Rhodesia.

Although the whole Rhodesian population is involved in these basic political struggles, it is probably true that those Africans living in areas nearest to the main urban centres have been most heavily exposed to the immediate consequences of every political act. Of the Shona-speaking peoples, the Zezuru, who live in the Salisbury region, have been most deeply involved.

But as will be shown in greater detail in chapter 4, the Zezuru of Chiota have been in the forefront of change ever since the beginnings of the colony of Southern Rhodesia. Waddilove Methodist Mission (then called Nenguo Mission) was established soon after the arrival of the Pioneer Column of 1890, in 1892 and the area was very much involved in the Shona Rebellion of 1896–7 when

16

the spirit-mediums co-ordinated various Shona chiefdoms (predominantly Zezuru) in their last-ditch attempt to rid their country of the white settlers. Since that time the people of Chiota have participated in no mean way to successive stages in Rhodesia's development, contributing notable preachers, teachers, businessmen and nationalist political leaders.

Against this background of rapid political and economic change, it may seem at first sight paradoxical that Chiota should also have become, in the early 1960s, a focus of 'traditional' religious activity centred around the cult of the spirit-mediums, and a region notorious for its valorisation of 'traditional' custom and values.

2

Magico-religious beliefs - the moral significance of explanation

At the same time that Chiota was rapidly incorporated into the political and economic structures developed in the colony of Southern Rhodesia, it was also incorporated into Christendom by the mission activities of the Methodists, Roman Catholics and Anglicans who set up churches and schools throughout the area. However, just as many 'tribal' institutions have survived this process, so have the old religious beliefs and practices. Indeed they have done more than merely survive; in recent years they have acquired a new relevance as part of a process of cultural regeneration which accompanied the rise of African nationalism.[1]

The main emphasis of this book is on the political significance of magico-religious beliefs and I have tended to stress the way in which beliefs are manipulated in concrete situations. Middleton, in his analysis of Lugbara religion, went so far as to claim that Lugbara 'have no set of interconsistent beliefs as to the nature of man and the world. Their beliefs are significant in given situations and their consistency lies in the way in which they are used in ritual action.' (Middleton 1960 : 25). The Lugbara and the Zezuru in common with most non-Islamic African societies are lacking in specialised theologians and their magico-religious beliefs are essentially practically orientated notions which are brought into play to account for the many unfortunate events thrown up in day-to-day life. However, this does not mean to say that they do not follow certain basic structural principles. Evans-Pritchard observed that it was impossible for any one Zande to describe his beliefs in witchcraft in their totality. 'It is no use saying to a Zande "Now tell me what you Azande think about witchcraft" because the subject is too general and indeterminate, both too vague and too immense to be described concisely. But it is possible to extract the principles of their thought from dozens of situations in which witchcraft is called upon to explain happenings and from dozens of other situations in which failure is attributed to some other cause.' (Evans-Pritchard 1937 : 70). In this chapter I set out to present an overview of Zezuru magico-religious beliefs and to show how they do have an inner consistency. To borrow Saussure's terminology, I set out first to examine the 'langue' of Zezuru beliefs and then, later, the 'parole'.

18

Magico-religious beliefs

The creator of the world

When the Christian missionaries arrived, they equated their own God with Mwari, who was also known by the epithets Musikavanhu (Creator of Men) and Wedenga (Of the Sky). Whether or not it was a suitable equation to make, Mwari is now regarded by most people as a universal High God, the supreme moral authority who created the world and is ultimately responsible for all that happens in it. He is in this sense as much the God of the white man as of the black, of the Shona as of the Ndebele.

However, the close personal relations which protestant Christianity emphasises between individual men and women and their God do not obtain in Chiota. Mwari, like most African supreme beings, is a distant figure whose supremacy is more theoretical than practical. Much more importance is attached to the spirits (*mwea*) who are believed to mediate between man and God, in much the same way as the saints do in folk catholicism. Indeed the Catholic missionaries made the parallel between their saints and the spirits of the Zezuru in their attempts to explain and further their own doctrine.

The spirits

The word *mwea* means either spirit, breath or personality. When a man dies, his personality becomes a spirit which continues to play a part in the social affairs of the living and which may 'come out' (*kubuda*) through a spirit-medium and so actually converse with living men.

The spirits are arranged in a hierarchy which is made up of two kinds of spirit, the *makombwe* (sing. *gombwe*), which I translate as heroes, and the *vadzimu*, or ancestor spirits.

The heroes occupy the highest echelons of the spirit hierarchy and are believed to be nearest to Mwari. They have authority over the ancestor spirits and mediate between them and God, and although they fall into the general category of spirit (*mwea*), they are sometimes referred to as *mhepo* which also means wind.

The seniority of the hero spirits is also an historical one, for they are believed to have lived on earth before the founding of Zezuru society in a region called Guruuswa to the north of the Zambezi river. Some of them are believed to have founded specific clans over which they exercise special authority. They differ from ordinary ancestor spirits in that their exact geneaologocal links with the living are not known.

Apart from this, there is very little information about the kinds of people the heroes were or what kind of society they lived in. Furthermore, when stories are told about them it is very often difficult to distinguish between events in which they themselves were involved and those in which their mediums played a part.

19

All spirits may possess living people who then act as their mediums and it will be shown in the following chapter how the powers of particular spirits are a function of the ability of their particular mediums. However it is sufficient to note at this stage that the hero spirits are believed to top the spirit hierarchy and as a result to have especial powers of healing, or prophecy and of rain-making. They are basically beneficent and care for the living, but their beneficence depends on the good behaviour of living men. The heroes uphold morality by withdrawing their protection when the living fail to obey their moral obligations to each other and with respect to the dead.

Below the hero spirits come the ancestor spirits, who are more directly concerned with the day-to-day affairs of their descendants.

When a man dies, three funerary rites are performed and they have the dual function of dealing with the distribution of the dead man's roles and possessions and with his transformation into an ancestor spirit. At the first rite, *guva*, the body is buried, his most personal effects (*nhumbi*) distributed and a regent appointed to take temporary control of his affairs. At the second rite of *kurova guva* (beating the grave), which takes place about a year after the first, his official successor is appointed and his property (*nhaka*) distributed. His spirit is 'brought back' and is installed as a fully fledged member of the lineage ancestral body. Between the first and second rites, his spirit is believed to roam around unattached and to have no voice in the running of lineage affairs. The only effect it can have on the living is to cause sickness as a sign that the second funerary rite is overdue. The third rite of *kudzururu guva* (smearing the grave) takes place some time later and represents the final consolidation of the dead man's spirit as a fully-fledged ancestor. The rite is of less significance than the first two, and I was not able to determine its specific function. It is generally held in response to sickness as a necessary formality.

The dead man's estate is divided into his personal effects (*nhumbi*) and the property which he controlled by virtue of his social position (*nhaka*). The former, which consists of small objects of personal use, such as clothes, his pillow, and pipes is scattered amongst his relatives by his senior sister's son (*muzukuru*), while the latter, which consists of his cattle, his wives and the debts and credits associated with the marriage payments of his daughters are inherited by the one person who also succeeds to the role he occupied as father of a family, head of a lineage or whatever. What is personal and idiosyncratic is scattered, what is due to his social structural position is inherited by a close agnatic relative, either a son or younger brother, according to the principles outlined in chapter 1.

The same principles that apply to property also apply to the dead man's spirit, for the transformation that takes place involves the sloughing off of any personal and idiosyncratic personality traits so that the ancestor spirit which is 'brought back' at the second rite is the dead man's personality bereft of any strictly individual characteristics. Although I found no overall unanimity on this point, many people agreed that individual personality traits hive off to become peripheral *shave* spirits which may attach themselves to relatives of the dead man, thus being scattered in the same way as his personal effects.

Ancestor spirits, then, are different from the personalities of living men. Devoid of essentially personal characteristics they represent the essence of what might be called structural personality. Their significance lies in their genealogical positions and the rights and duties which derive from them. They represent ideal men who, relieved of personal peculiarities and petty jealousies, are able to act as moral and just guardians of pure morality.

The society of the ancestors is a kind of ideal paradigm for Zezuru society as a whole, a society in which people behave without self-interest and enjoy their rights and obey their obligations defined by the ideals of descent and affinity.

In relation to the living, the ancestors are believed to exercise a protection which is vital, but, like the heroes, they may remove this protection as punishment should their descendants fail to live up to their social and ritual obligations. They insist that the living observe the ideals of correct social intercourse and that they perform regular rituals (*mapira*) at which they offer beer and dancing to their ancestors who commune with them through their chosen mediums. The ancestors are basically beneficent, so that their punishment is not direct, but when they withdraw their protection they leave open the door (*kuvura musuwo*) to disaster and the success of the evil manipulations of witches and sorcerers (*varoyi*), which will be discussed later in this chapter.

The heroes and the ancestors, then, are the moral bastions of Zezuru society whose continuance depends on their goodwill and protection. They stand essentially for the common good of the social groups of which they are the founders and this is given ritual expression in the communal rituals which are regularly held. The ancestors are on the side of group values and openness; free from purely personal interests they stand opposed to the machinations of those who would go against collective ideals and ignore their social obligations for reasons of jealousy or personal advancement.

Apart from the heroes and the ancestors, a third kind of spirit, *mashave* (sing. *shave*) tempers the rather uniform morality of the others. These spirits are not concerned with morality as such but are generally responsible for inoffensive individual differences between people, the kind of difference which makes life worth living but which does not threaten sacred values. Successful businessmen who deny the use of magical techniques often attribute their good fortune to *shave* spirits and excellent thumb-piano players claim that their talents are more than learned technique and derive from *shave* spirits. I heard stories of a remarkably adept thief whose skills were attributed to his association with a baboon spirit (*shave re gudo*).

Associated with the moral difference between the *shave* spirits and the ancestors and heroes is a fundamental structural difference, for whereas the latter are seen as being internal to Zezuru society, the former are believed to originate from outside it. They are 'outsiders' (*vatorwa*) and are the spiritual equivalent of the social and natural environment. Not only are baboon *shaves* found, but also Englishman *shaves* and Boer *shaves* who are the spiritual residue of non Zezuru who lived and died in Rhodesia. The heroes and the ancestors are within Zezuru society, and they exercise a moral authority over the groups which they articulate in structural terms and which they protect. The *shave* spirits come from outside. They are not associated with social groups, nor do they exercise moral control; they account for the special talents of individuals to whom they attach themselves quite arbitrarily.[2]

Included in the *shave* category, however, is a spirit which would appear not to confer inoffensive distinctiveness, but an entirely offensive power. The witching *shave* (*shave ro uroyi*) represents inherent evil.

Witchcraft

The Zezuru like the Azande distinguish between witchcraft and sorcery. The former applies to an inherent power to do harm by non-empirical means, while the latter is used with reference to those who consciously manipulate certain magical techniques to harm others.[3]

Zezuru witches are always women and they derive their powers from *shave* spirits which they inherit from their mothers, that is matrilineally. It is believed that a woman with such a witching *shave* may be possessed at night by her spirit which directs her to kill people and then to eat them. The witches of a village are believed to operate collectively in this way.

But as *shave* spirits act independently of human direction, the women who are possessed by them are not held personally responsible for the harm they cause, and it is possible for them to be exorcised by a competent spirit-medium. I suggest that the concept of witchcraft is a recognition of inherent evil in Zezuru society which is attributed to women because of their structural position and in recognition of the very real power that they wield in spite of their official status as jural minors.

In this patrilineal society, lineages depend for their continuity on the wives of lineage members; but because of the rules of exogamy, wives are brought in as 'outsiders' (*vatorwa*). They never change their lineage affiliation and the men of a lineage are distinguished not so much with reference to their fathers, as with reference to their mothers, each of which provides her sons with their own *matrilateral* relatives. Marriage regulations are such that a man may not marry a woman from his own lineage or clan, nor any woman with whom he can trace a blood relationship up to the sixth degree. In effect, then, men of the same lineage are distinguished from one another by the different circle of women they cannot marry and which is defined with reference to their mothers. Women as wives and mothers differentiate men of the same lineage where there is supposed to be the greatest homogeneity.[4]

But women do not simply symbolise differentiation within lineages; they may

actually encourage it and bring about disunity and fission. The bonds that develop between a mother and her children are often stronger than those which
unite all the children of one father or of brothers. As was shown in the previous
chapter this leads to a conflict of interests between lineage and matrisegment
interests and very often conflict between those whom custom commands to be
the greatest friends.

It is, of course, convenient for men to be able to conceal their own interper-
sonal animosities by blaming bad blood on their wives, and male informants
claimed that the word for a woman which is *mukadzi* was derived from either
muparadzi which means destroyer, or *mutadzi* which means sinner. Now that
men spend so much more time away from their villages working in the towns and
farms, women establish even stronger bonds with their children, and when they
themselves work for wages or brew beer for cash, they may begin to exercise an
economic control over them as well. It is tempting to see the beliefs in female
witchcraft operating in a similar way to that described by Nadel for the Nupe
where the menfolk whose authority is more imaginary than real consoled themselves on the mystical plane as the hunters of female witches.[5]

In the context of the present analysis, however, it is sufficient to note that
outsider spirits (*mashave*) are believed to possess outsider women who thus carry
the responsibility for the inherent evil in society. They do not *choose* to be
witches; they must accept, as a category, the responsibility for the structural
tensions generated by the rules of patrilineage exogamy in a male dominated
society. When men are accused of causing harm to others by magical means (or
by non-magical means in secret), however, it is an accusation of planned and conscious malice and the responsibility is personal.

Medicine, magic and sorcery

Any substance or technique which is used to bring about change in the human
condition, whether it be aspirin or a love potion made out of pubic hairs and
sweat, comes under the category of *muti* (pl. *miti*, this also means tree) or
mushonga. Those who employ these devices in secret and for selfish motives are
seen as sorcerers, and although the term *muroyi* is applied to witches as well, the
two concepts are clearly distinguished. Although pharmaceuticals and folk rem-
edies are not really classified as *uroyi* (sorcery), they are not entirely free from
moral taint, for it is held that were the rules of the ancestors to be wholly
obeyed there would be no suffering in the world and therefore no need for treatment. Indeed, many spirit-mediums refuse to have anything to do with any
medicine as it can so often cause as much harm as good.

What really makes medicine sorcery, then, is the way it is used. Anything that
is used publicly can be reckoned safe, but that which the individual does in private is always suspect.[6] The same word *muroyi* that is used for the witch and for
the sorcerer is also used metaphorically, for those who work secretly to bring

23

about harm either directly or indirectly to others. Thus the informer who is believed to have betrayed his kinfolk to the police may be called a *muroyi*.

Those *miti* which are classed unequivocally as *uroyi* are those that are supposed to be used for the express purpose of bringing harm to others. *Chipotswa* may be placed in the victim's pathway to bring pains to his legs, *chitsinga* at crossroads to bring pains to his joints, while one type of sorcery is believed to be concealed in the user's thumb nail to be dropped surreptitiously into his victim's beer.[7] One of the most dangerous types of sorcery is *gona*. Made out of the horn of an animal (*gona*), this medicine is believed to be able to be directed against the victim in order to kill him.

Futa is an interesting type of sorcery, for it is believed to be used in order to hamper spirit-mediumship. *Futa*, which also means 'fat', is administered to the novice medium and in impeding mediumship brings about sickness and maybe death to the victim in whose body the battle between the *futa* and the spirit which is trying to 'come out' (*kuduba*).

In all these cases of unequivocal sorcery, the medicines used require that the user obey certain 'rules' (*miko*, sing. *ruko*) which involve him in some kind of hardship. If he fails to obey them, then his sorcery will attack its owner instead of its intended victim. He must pay, with a certain amount of suffering, for the suffering which he is intending to cause in others. Indeed, the use of any kind of *muti* is expected to obey its rules on pain of paying for it with his own, or his close kin's suffering, for even medicine which is not used expressly to bring harm to others and yet which is used secretly is believed to bring about as much bad fortune as good to its owner.

There are certain types of *muti* which are designed to bring about justice where other methods have failed. *Meni* (lightning) is one of them and *chikwambo* another. The latter is generally used in land disputes and the exaction of marriage payments from recalcitrant sons-in-law. Its effects are various, but in one case a family which had refused to recognise the land rights of one of their kinsmen were plagued by stones which fell mysteriously through the thatched roof of their house until they gave way. When *meni* or *chikwambo* are used either when there is no case to answer or where other means have been tried and failed, they turn back on their owner who becomes the new victim.

Miti used for economic ends are legion, but the two most common are *divisi* which is used to ensure a good harvest and *mazango* which are good luck charms designed most commonly to bring about success in employment. Also it is believed that businessmen use specially powerful *miti* to guarantee the success of their businesses and these, like both *divisi* and *mazango*, have very harsh rules. When the bus of a well-known Chiota businessman ran over a small child it was not considered a mere accident. The child had to be killed as part of the business-medicines' rules. It is generally believed that the success of businessmen is balanced by misfortune in others, and such is the power that is accredited to

24

business magic that it can only be paid for by death. When its owner cannot kill a stranger, he may find his own kinsfolk dying in payment.

Even love potions (*mufuwhira*) have their hidden dangers and the woman who slips this into her lover's or her husband's food runs the risk of doing more harm than good. In sum, all medicine that is used in secret for essentially selfish ends is dangerous, and the harm that it causes is the price that society has to pay for jealousy, for if it were not for jealousy (*shanje*), the laws of the ancestors would be obeyed, rights would be enjoyed and obligations met to the mutual happiness of all. People are believed to resort to magical techniques in order to further their personal ambitions or to check the good fortune of others and the results are always disastrous.

But sorcery alone cannot be effective in bringing harm to its victim, for not even suffering or death can occur without the consent, albeit passive, of the ancestors and Mwari.

The choice of explanation

The ancestors are believed to look after their descendants as long as they conform to their social and ritual obligations. Ancestral protection is vital, for without it a person is vulnerable to the attacks of witches and sorcerers and to the vagaries of nature. In other words, for any misfortune a double explanation is required. First it is necessary to know which ancestor is angry and why and secondly who has employed magical techniques as a direct cause of the misfortune.

In any explanation of misfortune, therefore, the ancestors, who stand for collective ideals and morality, utilise the very forces to which they are most violently opposed, that is the egoistic striving of the jealous and greedy, to bring about their own justice. It is ironical that those who anger the ancestors for their failure to live up to collective ideals are allowed to be victims of others who are doing the same thing. In all senses it would appear that secret manipulation brings its just rewards.

But this is all very theoretical. In practice there is no such levelling out and the egalitarian ethic that this zero sum game implies is much more an ideal than a reality. Although the accounts are sometimes reckoned up to prove the case, it would be difficult to reconcile the patent disparities of good and bad fortune with the belief system which has just been described. While it might console the less fortunate to think that their more fortunate brethren will suffer in the long run, and while beliefs in witchcraft and sorcery might be invoked to try and discredit the super-ordinately successful, they are not strong enough to control the social differentiation which is a consequence of the kind of economic system which obtains in Southern Rhodesia. In effect the beliefs themselves control absolutely nothing; it is they which are controlled. With very few exceptions indeed, the physical nature of an event does not indicate its causes, which can only be assessed *ex post facto* after a careful analysis of the situation. For any given misfortune there are an infinite number of possible explanations and as long as it is reasonable to assume that witchcraft, sorcery and the ancestors are purely analytical concepts which cannot be empirically observed, the *choice* or *choices* of explanation will depend on factors other than the specific nature of the misfortune. But because all the beliefs which have been mentioned have strong moral connotations, the selection of explanation will be governed by political considerations. While one explanation might condemn A as a sorcerer, another might condone him as an ancestral favourite and so on. The coherence of Zezuru explanatory beliefs lies less in their totality than in their situational invocation. Zezuru magico-religious beliefs not only explain events, they also make moral statements about the persons involved in them.[8]

Kadiki was the eldest son of a large polygynous family and soon after his marriage which was financed by his father he left his village in Chiota to seek work on the European farms. For many years he did not return, ignoring his obligations to his wife, his in-laws, his family and his ancestors. He married on the farms and had three children, two sons and one daughter. But after some thirty years the farm on which he was working changed hands and Kadiki was sacked by the new owner on the grounds that he was too old to work efficiently. He was given a small 'pension' of £60 and left to his own devices. There was nowhere for him to go except his natal village to which he sent his daughter to ask permission to return. The reaction of his brothers was cold, for although as eldest brother he had rights to live and farm in the village, he had so ignored his obligations that his return was not welcome. However he was given a place to build a house and a field to farm.

Shortly after returning, his daughter became sick. Speculation was rife as to the cause of her sickness but the general consensus of the villagers was that the sickness was somehow due to the fact that the ancestors had withdrawn their protection from Kadiki because he had ignored them for so long and had not even returned for his father's funeral. This interpretation was confirmed by a herbalist/diviner (*nganga*) whom Kadiki consulted and he was commanded to brew beer for a ritual (*bira*) for the ancestors. The direct cause of the affliction was attributed to one of Kadiki's daughter's lovers. Apparently she had taken a number of lovers on the farms and had been married to at least one of them. When he had paid a portion of the agreed bridewealth to Kadiki and came to claim his wife, she had refused to go. The villagers agreed with the *nganga*'s verdict that this lover had worked *muti* (medicine) against her.

Kadiki bought the grain for the beer and had it brewed and invited the whole family to the ritual. There he was obliged to make a public apology to the lineage ancestors who were present in their mediums, Kadiki's father's brother's daughter and another father's brother's son. However the sickness did not abate and by the time that Kadiki's £60 had been spent on living and on paying *nganga*'s fees there was nothing more that he could do.

26

Magico-religious beliefs

This is an example of the way in which beliefs are chosen in practice, and of the double explanation that is required. In this case Kadiki's weak economic and political position in the village meant that he had little choice but to accept the explanation that put moral guilt on his shoulders. He was forced to atone for his error by making what amounted to a public confession of guilt which cost him dearly not only in pride. Had he been in a stronger political and financial position it might have been possible for him to have opted for a different kind of explanation, but his position of dependence in the village obliged him to accept the majority view. When Kadiki's daughter did not get better general opinion in the village held that things had gone too far and that Kadiki's sins were too serious to be atoned for.

This explanation of Kadiki's plight was reached by a process of gossip and discussion followed by the pronouncement of a qualified magico-religious expert, the *nganga*. Although it is probably true to say that in most cases of affliction the *nganga*'s or the spirit-medium's pronouncement is a foregone conclusion for reasons which will be explored in the following chapter, only after a ritual expert has made an official divination can the chosen explanation be acted upon. Once this has happened mere suspicions are transformed into sacred edicts; *vox populi* becomes *vox dei*.

The ritual experts

Herbalist/diviners (*nganga*) generally claim to derive their powers from their association with a *shave* spirit which enables them to interpret the meaning of the carved wooden tablets (*hakata*) or other mechanical device[9] which they use in divination. They do not fall into a trance and they contact the ancestors and other spirits through the lie of their apparatus. *Ngangas* tend to operate in private with their clients, and they do not hold public rituals. Furthermore they not only divine into the causes of affliction but also prescribe medicinal cures for it. They are of ambiguous moral standing, for it is believed that the *miti* that they handle may be used for harm as well as good and it is from the *nganga* that the sorcery described above is supposed to be acquired.

Spirit-mediums operate according to quite different principles. They fall into trance and become possessed by their spirit, either an ancestor spirit or a hero and are able to divine on the principle that all spirits are in constant communication with all other spirits. They tend to divine in public at formal seances and they eschew the use of medicine in favour of purely ritual techniques. As long as a spirit-medium has public support, he is regarded as the paragon of moral virtue in contradistinction to his rival the *nganga*. The openness of the spirit-medium, his association with the ancestors and heroes which are the pillars of collective morality and his rejection of medicines which are morally tainted is in sharp contrast to the *nganga* whose secrecy and involvement with medicine associate him symbolically with those who work against collective ideals, the sorcerers.

These salient differences between the *nganga* and the spirit-medium, who both divine for the causes of misfortune demonstrate the same kinds of oppositions that have been established in the magico-religious beliefs on which they draw.

Conclusions

The competence of Zezuru magico-religious beliefs to explain extra-ordinary events and at the same time to make moral statements and to serve political ends in their situational invocation are revealed by looking at the same phenomenon from two points of view, the folk (emic) and the analytic (etic).

From the folk point of view the social world is divided up into various mutually inclusive categories, each of which is composed of an empirical and a non-empirical part. Mwari or God heads the most inclusive segment of all, the whole world, which is then divided up into Shona and non-Shona. The non-Shona (including nature) are made up of the observable world and of the *shave* spirits, while the Shona consist of the various clans which are linked to the hero spirits. The clans are further subdivided into lineages of differing span and depth which are articulated by the ancestor spirits. Permeating the whole system are the forces that may be unleashed by the use of medicine (*muti*).

The heroes and the ancestors, who are from this point of view within Shona society, are free spirits who may not be manipulated by the living. They lavish a benign protection on their descendants but withdraw it as punishment for moral fault. They are the guardians of the moral order. The *shave* spirits come from outside. They are also not manipulable by the living, but they are if anything amoral. They are responsible for individual talents and idiosyncrasies and also for the inherent evil in society which is passed on as witching *shaves* from mothers to their daughters.

Opposing the collective ideals are the medicines which may be manipulated by those whose motives spring from greed and envy (*shanje*) to thwart the ancestral ideal. Such people work characteristically in secret.

The oppositions between the heroes and ancestors and medicine, which are mediated by the *shave* spirits are summarised in table 1.

It would appear, then, that Zezuru magico-religious beliefs play upon the basic theme of the relationship between the individual and society putting a strong emphasis on the subordination of the former to the latter while at the same time allowing him a certain amount of room for manoeuvre. Even if the ideal is a clockwork society based on the mutual rights and duties defined by a patrilineal kinship structure, the reality is very different and demonstrates a marked diversity of personality and social behaviour which can be condoned by appeal to the notion of *shave* spirits or condemned by the concept of sorcery.

From the observer's point of view a rather different but nevertheless complementary picture emerges. Starting from the assumption that heroes, ancestors, *shave* spirits and sorcery have the status of theoretical concepts and not of proven

Magico-religious beliefs

Table 1

Heroes and ancestors	*Shave* spirits	Medicine (*muti*)
Associated with groups	Associated with individuals and categories	Associated with individuals
Morality (collective ideals)	Amorality (inevitable individual idio-syncrasy)	Immorality (selfish striving)
Inside	Outside	?
Rituals open and public	Rituals open and public	Rituals secret
Not manipulable	Not manipulable	Manipulable
Spirit-mediums	Herbalist/diviners (*nganga*)	

facts, it follows that the whole gamut of beliefs is manipulable by the people who invoke them. From this point of view the ancestors are as manipulable as medicine. The choice of a particular explanation can only be understood in relation to its socio-political context. While for the actor, explanations of misfortune are truths revealed by a ritual expert with all the certainty of causal sequences that this implies, from the observer's point of view explanations are arrived at *ex post facto* on the basis of their political aptitude. No explanation is 'true' in a scientific sense; it can only be interpreted as significant in relation to a given social situation.

3

The sociology of spirit-mediumship

The Theory of Spirit-mediumship

It is believed that any male spirit (*mwea*) may come out (*kubuda*) through a
living person who becomes its medium (*svikiro*). While the medium is possessed
(*kusvikirwa*, lit. arrived on), his body acts as a 'pocket' (*homwe*) for the spirit
and during this period of trance his own personality (*mwea*) is absent. All that
occurs during trance is directed by the possessing spirit and when the medium
returns to normality he is ignorant of all that has taken place during trance. I
have therefore adopted the terminology suggested by Firth (1959 : 141), who
defined spirit possession as 'a form of trance in which the behaviour patterns of
a person *are interpreted as* evidence of a control of his behaviour by a spirit ex-
ternal to him' and spirit mediumship as 'a form of possession in which the person
is conceived as serving as an intermediary between spirits and men. The accent
here is on communication; the actions and words of the mediums must be trans-
latable, which differentiates them from mere spirit possession or madness.' The
italics are my own and emphasise that these definitions are based on what the
actors believe and not on any 'scientific' criteria.[1]

The making of a medium

When a spirit wishes to come out through a medium for the first time, it is believed to cause the person concerned a certain amount of hardship. Any sickness,
therefore, could be interpreted as being due to this cause. However this is one of
the few exceptions to the rule that physiological symptoms do not in themselves
indicate their cause,[2] for allergies to such things as African beer, tobacco smoke,
and petrol fumes are generally believed to herald spirit-mediumship. In the event
of these symptoms occurring, or another misfortune which might be appropri-
ately interpreted in terms of imminent spirit-mediumship, the patient is taken to
either an established spirit-medium or a herbalist/diviner (*nganga*) for
confirmation.

   If the suspicions of a group or person are confirmed by divination, then
efforts are made to achieve spirit-possession followed by mediumship. It is believed that the misfortune will continue until such time as mediumship has been
achieved.

   The normal course of action to bring about possession is to hold a *bira* ritual.

30

The noun *bira* (pl. *mapira*) is derived from the verb *kupira* which means literally to give to (*kupa* is 'to give'). So, in essence, *mapira* are occasions of sacrifice to the ancestors. (*Tirikupira vadzimu vedu*: we are sacrificing to our ancestors). They may be held for many purposes, such as for opening a new *banya* (seance house) for a 'high-level' medium, or for giving beer to the spirits of a kin group if this has been divined as being the cause of some misfortune in the group, but the general pattern is the same. Essentially they are formalised seances during which a group of persons holds commerce with the spirits through mediums in trance.

Organisation of a *bira* is complex, even if it is only for a small kin group and its ancestors. The brewing of beer takes seven days and considerable labour from the collecting of firewood to the final dishing-up on the last day. Guests have to be invited, such as mediums living close by, the *mbira* players, matrilateral relatives of the new medium and representatives of his affines. Expenses are comparatively heavy. *Mbira* players charge about £3 a night, the beer may be upwards of £2 10s 0d in value, and, if an established 'high-level' medium is invited to assist in order to sponsor the new medium then his transport costs will have to be met as well as his fees which may be as much as ten pounds. It is an important principle that none of the expenses incurred in the bringing out of a new medium may be borne by the medium himself, but rather by his close kin or friends. If the medium were to finance himself, it would appear that he was trying to 'buy off' the spirits, (*anange arikutenga vadzimu*).

Mapira usually take place on Saturdays so that those members of kin groups who work in town may be able to be present (they are also relied upon for help with the expenses), and as night falls, the company gathers in the house for the first beer (*musumo* – from *kusuma* – to announce), which is presented to the spirits who are notified as to the nature of the business. At this stage the village headman invites all present to restrain themselves while drinking, to keep the peace and to refrain from making use of the dark to drop poison in other peoples' beer.

After the drinking of *musumo*, the *mbira* start playing and dancing commences, with intermittent pauses for more beer. Very soon, the heat generated in the house, the insistant rhythm of the rattles (*magosho*), the melismatic tinkling of the upper register of the *mbira* over the inexorable passacaglia-like melodies of the lower, sometimes reinforced by the bass drone of the men, the ululation of the women and the clapping of hands on the cross rhythm join with the dust thrown up by the pounding feet of the dancers in bringing on trance. The first mediums to fall into trance are the already established ones. Characteristically they are 'gripped' (*kudunzwa*) by their spirits, so that their dancing becomes the more frenzied until they are thrown to the ground (*kukandwa pasi*) where they sit still jerking to the sound of the music and roaring like lions.[3] When the music stops and beer is drunk conversations are held with the spirits present. Although the spirits are treated as superiors, the patterning of their relationship with men is modelled on the *sekuru/muzukuru* (grandfather/grandchild or mother's brother/sister's son) relationship, so that there is considerable respect coupled with familiarity and friendship. Spirit presentations are addressed as *Vasekuru* (honoured grandfather), while men are addressed by the spirits as *vazukuru* (grandchild).

Established mediums usually fall into trance quite easily, but the first trance of a new medium has to be achieved by the conscious effort of all those present, who are expected to dance fervently in return for the beer that they are given. The *mbira* players for their part, work their thumbs to the bone to bring about trance as they are judged on their ability to do so. If all goes well, the new medium is 'gripped' and, like the other mediums, falls to the ground in the characteristic manner. The music stops, and the new medium/spirit is asked by the senior spirit-medium present to disclose his name and parentage. He is then expected to give his own personal name, the name of his father and the clan name (*chidawo*) of his mother, thus establishing his precise genealogical status. If all present consider this information to be satisfactory and true, then that is taken as *prime facie* evidence of the genuineness of the trance state. The recognition given by the important spirit-medium who has been invited serves to legitimise the status of the new medium in a wider sense.

The *bira* continues with intermittent dancing, singing, beer-drinking and discussions between the living and the dead as presented by the mediums. As the sun rises, the final beer (*maradzo* — from *kuparadza* — to disperse) is brought out and drunk. After this the mediums usually depart into the bush and return, no longer in trance, eager to hear what has passed in their absence during the night. The ritual is now over and the people move away leaving only close kin who stay behind for breakfast which either takes the form of tea and bread or else another pot of beer.

Although the accomplishment of trance and the first words of the new medium are *prima facie* evidence of genuine possession, the new medium is not yet complete in his status. There remains a further *bira* concluded by the ordeal of *kudya muropa*. The *bira* is conducted as before, except that at dawn the new medium is led outside, in trance, and shown an animal (either an ox or a goat) whose throat is then slit by a *muzukuru* (sister's son) of the new medium. The blood (*ropa*) is gathered in a wooden bowl and the medium, still in trance, drinks it, grabs a knife, slits open the chest of the animal and eats the liver (*chiropa*) and breast flesh. The more avid the spirit appears to be, then the stronger is believed to be the possession. Again this ordeal is treated in a very matter-of-fact way, and the ordinary people present joke with the new spirit, pleading that it might not eat all the meat raw, and that it might leave some over for them to eat later. In some cases it is forcibly restrained and the rest of the meat is then distributed amongst those present for cooking and subsequent consumption.

The effectiveness of this ordeal lies in the belief that the consumption of raw flesh and blood by ordinary people is fatal. The mere survival of the spirit-medium is regarded as proof that he was possessed at the time of the ordeal and that it was not he who ate the meat, but the spirit.

The process described above is as it happens ideally (we shall see later that this ideal pattern is not so often achieved in practice), and can be interpreted as a *rite de passage* through which the community and the neophyte himself re-adjust to a new configuration of social roles. The new medium has been accepted by the community of persons involved and the final ordeal has declared him duly genuine. From the actors' point of view it is tempting to accept Fortes' view (1962 : 86) that, 'Through ritual, office is presented to the holder in a binding manner, or again, conversely, legitimately stripped from him. Ritual presents office to the individual as the creation and possession of society into which he is to be incorporated through office. Ritual mobilises incontrovertible authority behind the granting of office and status and thus guarantees its legitimacy and imposes accountability for its proper exercise.' However, this ritual sequence cannot be taken as the final word on the matter. The medium must continue to satisfy the community if he is to continue to receive its support. These *rites de passage* are a necessary but not sufficient condition for ensuring the legitimacy of spirit-mediums. At one seance, I witnessed a significant change of opinion in a small group of kin. The divining medium suggested that the man whom they had all up until then held to be the medium of one of their agnatic ancestors was not genuine and that in fact it was his younger brother who should have been medium. When one of their number noted that he had gone through the ordeal of *kudya muropa*, the ensuing discussion enabled them to recollect that he had not really eaten very much or with much vigour.

In this case, then, what Fortes calls the 'incontrovertible authority' which ritual mobilises is not incontrovertible at all; it must, and does, give way to the truly incontrovertible authority which is public opinion. Although the ritual involved in the induction of new mediums may be effective in reordering relevant social relations, such is the nature of spirit-mediumship that its effectiveness can only be temporary, for, as will shortly be seen, mediums may subsequently be dismissed as frauds, downgraded or even elevated in status. Just as a Melanesian craftsman cannot hope simply to manufacture a beautiful arm shell or necklace and expect it to take on the status of a prestige Kula valuable, neither can a Zezuru man or woman expect to be acclaimed as a powerful medium simply through being 'made' by the prescribed ritual techniques. Until he has proved himself a capable medium, until he has attracted many clients and unless he can satisfy the expectations of those clients, his status is precarious.

This point is so important that it will be necessary to return later to discuss the ways in which mediums may be discredited. First, however, I continue to describe the formal properties of the system.

The spirit-medium's role

Spirit-mediums fall into two broad categories, the high-level and the low-level mediums. The former are hosts to either hero spirits or very senior ancestor spirits, while the latter act as hosts to junior ancestors. This difference is apparent from the different cloths which they wear during trance. The high-level mediums wear wholly black cloths and the low-level ones half black, half white. The presence of white in the low-level mediums' cloths was interpreted by one informant as symbolising their having lived since the arrival of the whites in Rhodesia.

High-level mediums differ from low-level ones in style and scale. The former, if they are popular and successful, carry out their seances in large seance houses (*banya*), are surrounded by an administrative staff to take care of operations and to look after those who come to consult. They may reach the stage when they have to abandon all other activities and are then able to maintain themselves and their followers on the income derived from the fees which the clients are charged. The more popular the medium, the more well-known and powerful his spirit, the higher the fees and the larger is the scale of operations.

Low-level mediums, on the other hand, do not have seance houses and only fall into trance from time to time or at the occasional formal rituals which are held by their lineage groups for their ancestor spirits. They do not generally receive clients from beyond the confines of village or lineage and do not charge fees.

Although the high-level mediums are credited with greater powers than the low-level ones (only the former are able to make rain and to prophesy) the basic function of all mediums is that of divination. On the strength of the belief that all spirits are omniscient and in contact with one another, mediums in trance are supposed to be able to know the reasons for all misfortune. At divinatory seances they are expected to reveal the causes of affliction to their clients.

But because people go to a medium for divination with some idea of what they expect to hear, the medium is obliged to find out what this is and to present the 'truth' to his clients as divine revelation. If he fails, then the disappointed clients can ignore the 'wrong' pronouncement by claiming that the medium was not in trance, or – and this was very common – that the witchcraft involved in the misfortune was so powerful that it had affected the divining powers of the medium. In either case a 'wrong' pronouncement is a blow to a medium's prestige; reputation being won and lost on the ability to divine 'correctly'.

Divination, like many of the spirit-mediums' functions is half way between art and science. The spirit-medium has to size up the situation and produce, *ex cathedra* an explanation of his clients' misfortune which is acceptable to them.

David/*Kafudzi*, as a high-level medium, had a sizeable administrative staff, one of whose duties was to receive and care for clients as they arrived. Undoubtedly a certain amount of relevant information that emerged from these prior contacts with the clients was passed on to the medium and he entered the seance with this and other information that he might have gleaned from ordinary gossip or prior consultations. By and large, however, he had to start the divination from scratch and produce his analysis of the situation without appearing to use non-mystical techniques.

David/*Kafudzi*'s divinatory technique was based to a large extent on his empirical awareness of the regularities of Zezuru social structure. Due to the great number of divinations which he had carried out he was aware of the structural tensions in Zezuru society and on the basis of this knowledge he was able to predict tensions in particular situations which appeared to his clients as miraculous insight. This interpretation is supported by the way in which seances were conducted. Clients were instructed to sit facing the spirit-medium according to their genealogical relationships. Men sat to his right as fathers, brothers, . . . while the women sat to his left as sisters, mothers and wives . . .

The eldest man present was asked to explain why they had come to divine and his reasons were translated by an acolyte into the language which David/*Kafudzi* spoke (see below p. 41). David /*Kafudzi* would then suggest a relationship of tension between two of the people before him, say a woman and her sister-in-law or a pair of brothers. If he succeeded in exposing a tension that really existed and was relevant to the situation, then the reaction of his clients was usually sufficiently obvious for him to be able to pursue this particular line of enquiry. It sometimes happened that such preliminary questions produced no results, in which case he generally resorted to asking the women one by one which had been using love potions (*mufuwhira*). This exploitation of inter-sexual tensions nearly always evinced enthusiasm amongst the men and frequently led to elaborate confessions on the part of those women who were forced by the general consensus into making them. David/*Kafudzi* surely realised either that all women use *mufuwhira* or that even if they don't they can be forced into confessing to it when sufficiently cajoled.[4] From the point of view of the clients, however, David/*Kafudzi*'s socio-psychological insights were perceived as divine revelations. Impressed by the medium's divinatory powers, clients were generally maneouvred into giving away more than they realised about themselves and about what they had been thinking in relation to their problems, so that the medium was able to reach the kind of explanation that they had previously had in mind.

David/*Kafudzi* and other mediums, then, exploited what they knew about social tension and the symbolic meaning of dress and gesture to explain misfortune. Contented clients left the seance convinced of the truth of what they had heard, willing and ready to carry out the ritual injunctions prescribed as necessary for the alleviation of their misfortunes.

Evans-Pritchard (1937 : 170) makes very similar observations in relation to Zande diviners, noting how they make use of their knowledge of local scandal and of their understanding of 'the stock enmities in Zande culture' in order to divine successfully. 'A witch-doctor divines successfully because he says what his listener wishes him to say, and because he uses tact.' While Evans-Pritchard pays special attention to these and other 'technical' prerequisites of successful divination he does not exclude the importance of the diviner's intuition, in this case enhanced by music and dance. Similarly in the case of the Zezuru it would be difficult to deny that many mediums, through the experience of trance, do acquire insights which would escape them in more 'ordinary' states of mind. Furthermore, when dealing with such a little understood area of human behaviour as trance, it would be out of place to attempt a total explanation in terms of standard sociological paradigms.

From the discussion so far it might appear that Zezuru spirit-mediums are devoted servants of their community and clients, working hard to solve other people's problems and working constantly towards hallowed community goals. Indeed this is exactly the way in which spirit-mediums present themselves. For them, spirit-mediumship is a difficult calling. Dancing, trance and long seances are tiring and there are many neophyte mediums who profess a great distaste for their calling, which they feel to be a duty to their spirits and to the community.

The compensation in spirit-mediumship — status and prestige

But spirit-mediumship is not all give and no take; there are compensations even though they are not explicit in the belief system. According to the rules, spirit-mediums are tools of their spirits. When they are in trance their own personalities give way to the incoming spirit and are therefore irrelevant. A consequence of this theory is that spirit-mediums enjoy the status of their spirits only during trance, and in ritual contexts. When out of the ritual context they have no more duties and privileges than ordinary people. Furthermore, any 'gifts' that are given by grateful clients are the property of the spirit and not of the medium. Any income from seances may only be used, therefore, for the well-being of the spirit for buying cloths or ritual paraphanalia, or for buying food for destitute clients.

The real picture, however, is very different. Mediums *do* enjoy considerable social prestige even when out of trance, and many mediums dress all the time in black shirts so that their status may be easily identified.[5] When two Zezuru men meet one another, the more junior claps hands *ku-uchira*) to the more senior and initiates the greeting sequence. I very rarely saw a medium initiate such a greeting even to the most esteemed members of the community, whether priests, chiefs, teachers or businessmen. Although this fact appears to contradict the belief that mediums out of trance revert to their ordinary statuses, it is possible to justify what actually happens by referring to the belief that mediums are chosen on the basis of their moral qualities (*hana*). The respect shown to spirit-mediums can be said to be not for the spirit, but for the moral worth of the medium which caused the spirit to choose him as host in the first place.

Much the same kind of thing happens with regard to the income of spirit mediums, who may be able to divert a certain quantity of cash to their own private ends on the basis that the spirit requires its host to be fit and healthy in order that he might continue to act as a strong medium. However, mediums who divert too much cash in to their own pockets run the risk of being suspected of selfish motives and subsequent discrediting. Furthermore, and I shall return to this point shortly, the ambitious medium knows that one of the best ways of winning friends and influencing people is to give gifts. Mediums gain popularity and maintain it by being generous with their money and by feeding and clothing indigent clients and destitute disciples. Much of their power derives from their position as controllers of redistributive systems.

For certain people, ambitious for status and prestige and (as will be seen later) a certain amount of political power, spirit-mediumship is an admirable profession. The compensations would appear at least to balance the effort if not exceed it; perhaps all the complaints about difficulties are part of a wider strategy to give even greater value to their work.

But what sort of people become spirit-mediums?

The 'epidemiology' of spirit-mediumship

In theory, the spirits choose their mediums, and they choose them on moral criteria alone. Spirit-mediumship is open to all people regardless of age, sex or genealogical status. However, it is clear that sociologically speaking, spirit-mediumship is an achieved status as opposed to the more ascribed statuses of chiefship and headmanship.[6] It is tempting to suggest, therefore, that spirit mediums might be recruited from the ranks of those who are for reasons of their sex, age or genealogical status, deprived of the possibility of secular office.

In point of fact, none of the ninety or so mediums I encountered were eldest sons, and approximately half were women, but the difficulty of accounting for this in terms of deprivation theory is twofold. In the first place, it would be necessary to show that spirit-mediums were persons structurally excluded from *all* other prestige positions such as teachers, priests, businessmen. This would be a daunting undertaking, and it would be difficult to take account of the cases where mediums had abandoned prestige jobs in order to become mediums or where mediums combined their mediumship with their jobs as teachers. But the second difficulty with deprivation theory is the more serious, for any explanation of social action founded on relative deprivation is bound to fall into tautology. Basic to the concept of relative deprivation is the idea that social strategies derive from a feeling of legitimate deprivation in relation to the past, other social groups and so on. However, all social action is legitimated in relation to felt needs and it goes without saying that the sociologist will have little difficulty in detecting other 'needs' *a posteriori*.

Another more satisfactory explanation for the preponderance of women and younger sons relates to their structural status as 'outsiders'. Women, and to a lesser extent younger sons, are excluded from hereditary office. They are therefore partially liberated from the most partisan positions in situations of family strife. Because spirit-mediums, and advice givers in general[7] are persons who are structurally 'outside' in relation to the people to whom they are giving advice, it would seem that younger brothers and women would be more suitable candidates than elder brothers. This applies especially to women who, because of the virilocal marriage norm, tend to be geographical outsiders as well. It might also be added that women qualify for spirit-mediumship with the added advantage of being rather better informed than men. Due to labour migration, men spend much of their time out of Chiota, while the women, as permanent residents, remain continuously *au fait* with local developments.

Unfortunately the lack of statistical data on the social characteristics of spirit-mediums does not make it possible for me to speculate further as to the kinds of social grooves[8] in which spirit-mediumship runs. Relying on observation and intuition, however, it can be suggested that spirit-mediumship, as Zezuru theory would have it, is, in fact, scattered through various social categories. It can in no way be correlated with any kind of mental disturbance; indeed one of the ways of discrediting a spirit-medium is to suggest that he is in some way 'mad'. On the contrary, spirit-mediums tend to be amongst the most intelligent and perceptive members of the community. Those who succeed as spirit-mediums and reach the highest levels require great skills and the ambition necessary to hold their own in a highly competitive area. The history of David Mudiwa is a case in point.

David/*Kafudzi*

David Mudiwa was born in a village in Chiota in 1930. After being educated up to Standard III at a methodist primary school, he became a house painter working in Salisbury. During this time he became interested in religion and after a brief flirtation with the Vapostore sect,[9] entered the Methodist Church as an evangelist. He was so successful as a preacher that his congregation was able to raise sufficient funds to build a small chapel on the outskirts of his village.

Towards the end of 1963 he began to suffer from chronic stomach pains and to go into wild frenzies while preaching; so wild, in fact, that the congregation had to chain him down. His condition worsened and through dreams he was led to visit a spirit-medium in Zwimba Reserve. There he was told that he was being troubled by a spirit which wished to make him its medium. Rituals were held in Zwimba and David became possessed by three spirits, *Kafudzi* which was described as a water spirit (*nzuzu*); an obscure hero spirit related to the clan of hero spirits belonging to the Nyandoro clan; and the ancestor of David's father's father's father. He returned to his village where he built a small seance house on the top of a slight hill overlooking the methodist chapel.

It is at this stage in David's career as a medium that I first met him in April of 1965. He no longer held any church services and the chapel was being used as a guest house for the clients who had begun to consult him as a spirit-medium.

The sociology of spirit-mediumship

Apparently people had at first been rather confused by his change of status from methodist evangelist to spirit-medium, but after a short time the quality of his divination and his reputation as a healer brought him ever more consultants.

Soon business was so brisk that he was obliged to build a bigger and better seance house and was able to increase his fee from 5s to 10s and upwards depending on the nature of the problem. There gathered in David's village a small administrative nucleus made up for the most part of people who had been indicated as new spirit-mediums and who were undergoing ritual treatment. This staff looked after clients as they arrived and took care of the premises. David bought a car in order to be able to visit sick people and paid two excellent thumb-piano players to provide the music for his seances.

David/*Kafudzi* soon became especially noted for his ability to detect witches and sorcerers, for exorcising witching spirits (*shave ro uroyi*) and for his skill in 'bringing out' new spirits in those he had identified as potential spirit-mediums. The village was now full of sick people seeking cures, young men and women undergoing ritual treatment as neophyte mediums and women waiting to be possessed by their witching spirits that they might later have them exorcised. At weekends, the village was inundated with people from Salisbury who came by bus and car to consult on all manner of problems, ranging from money and employment difficulties to impotency, from severe sickness to the loss of relatives. As satisfied clients returned to their villages or to the towns, David's reputation increased and his sphere of influence expanded. Those who had come in order to become spirit-mediums returned to their villages and set up their own practices, but they maintained contact with David, and spread his fame even further.

By the end of 1966 David's reputation was almost as high as, if not higher than the mediums of well-established hero spirits in Chiota like *Biri na Ganiri* and *Chitswachegore*, and *Kafudzi*'s status as a water spirit had also improved. It would be difficult to pin-point this change in status, but imperceptibly *Kafudzi* became a hero with a complex history and a wealth of detail about his previous mediums. David/*Kafudzi* enjoyed telling this history; of how *Kafudzi* had been a member of the Vatemani clan which had lived before the formation of Shona society at a place called Guruuswa to the north of the river Zambesi; of how he had possessed mediums in other parts of the world, one in Dar-es-Salaam and another, a 'hindu' who had lived in the Himalayas. Visitors to the seance house were treated to more elaborate details and descriptions of the geography of the Himalaya mountains.

By the time that I left the field in 1966 the followers of David did not remember that *Kafudzi* had ever been a mere water spirit. History had been made.

Of course there remained pockets of opposition in Chiota, notably amongst the followers of other mediums and, as will be seen from the extended case history in chapter 5, there were those who were able to regard him as a mere upstart and to ignore his pronouncements. But in spite of such opposition his success was remarkable.

Spirits of protest

In trying to understand David's success, it is possible to discern elements
which have a purely personal nature and lie beyond the scope of sociology and
others which are more technical and which might indicate a number of generalis-
ations about the way in which spirit-mediums acquire popularity. It is with the
latter that I am immediately concerned.

David Mudiwa, in common with most of the spirit-mediums of Chiota, was
riding on the crest of a wave of cultural nationalism which was sweeping that
region of Rhodesia at the time. There is no doubt that the mood of the people
was propitious for his particular brand of spirit-mediumship; his ritual emphasis
on witchcraft and the induction of new spirit-mediums, his constant appeals to
'traditional' values and his subtle use of certain African nationalist symbols were
an important aspect of his success. This aspect of spirit-mediumship in Chiota
will be examined in greater detail in chapter 6, but it is sufficient to note at this
stage that David had been a methodist evangelist and his move over to spirit-
mediumship reflected the general religious trends of the time.

More particularly, David was a good diviner, he knew how to use the income
that he earned from his seances to increase his popularity, and he was able to
augment his sphere of influence noticeably due to the emphasis he laid on 'training' new spirit-mediums.

I have already described his divinatory technique, so on this there is little to
add. He succeeded in offering the kinds of analysis that his clients wanted and
which they were able to accept. As far as cash income was concerned, he was
particularly astute. At first all the money (and on some weekends he earned upwards of £400) was put to specifically communal use. The seance house was
built, food was provided for visitors from long distances, thumb-piano players
were paid and houses and shelters were built for the neophyte spirit-mediums
and administrative staff. Very poor clients were not always charged while those
who could afford to pay more were expected to do so. The money was not used
for personal grandisement and the more money that was used for other people
the more David's popularity increased, for he was soon surrounded by a number
of people who could only repay him with loyalty.

Latterly he began to use his cash to start a retail business and to build a luxur-
ious house for his two wives. There were hints of criticism of this behaviour,
which never became really serious because he employed his friends and relatives
as workers and continued to be generous to others.

His policy on new spirit-mediums was particularly important. Young men and
women who had been told they were to be mediums stayed in his village upwards
of a year. They enjoyed his hospitality and attended his seances, contributing
with any help they could give. Bit by bit, as their spirits began to 'come out',
they absorbed the ritual techniques and learned their calling. Even though there
is no place for learning in Zezuru belief (for the spirits are believed to be all-
knowing), the neophyte mediums saw David's village as a school. When the time
came to return to their home villages, the new mediums kept in touch with

David, who would be invited to preside over any important rituals they might enact. They built their own seance houses and began to do as their master had done, even 'bringing out' their own disciple mediums. By this process, David, who remained at the centre of the network, acquired steadily more and more faithful adherents.

In a sense, all these techniques could be learned and applied by any spirit-medium. But they are all difficult and few are the spirit-mediums who have achieved David's success. The personal element is much more difficult to pin down.

Zezuru spirit-mediums are dramatic figures, and much of their fame is derived from the way in which they conduct themselves both in the ritual context and outside. David, even when out of the ritual context, left no doubt of his spirit-medium status. Apart from using a black shirt, he generally travelled with his musicians and an imposing sword stick (*bakatwa*). He carried an air of authority and importance.

But it was his ritual performance which earned him his greatest fame. The seance house was of exaggerated proportions and its dark interior was awesome. On entering it was possible to discern little, but as one's eyes became accustomed to the gloom it was possible to perceive the designs of lions and other animals picked out on the mud walls, and the many large black cloths which festooned the rafters. Opposite the main door was a pile of black cloths and animals' skins, on which would be seated a few neophyte mediums all in black. To their left were the musicians. Behind them a small door led to a sort of antechamber from which David emerged. As he entered the music became more energetic and he and his disciples rose to dance. In essence, the dance was not so different from modern western pop dancing; it was highly expressive and individualistic, allowing for extemporisation on a basic foot-pounding rhythm. During the dance *Kafudzi* would 'arrive' and, with the cessation of the music, the seance proper would begin.

David/*Kafudzi* did not speak ChiShona, but a language which, it was believed, had been the language of the Vatemani clan. This language was based on a simplified Shona grammar with a changed vocabulary whose words tended to have a wider semantic field than ChiShona ones. The medium's disciples all had a competence in this language, but clients did not. The latter could only talk with David/*Kafudzi* through an interpreter, which created an even greater respect for the powers of the medium. This language had a further important function in accentuating the mutual solidarity of those who could understand it.

All these aspects of David/*Kafudzi*'s performance, and others which it is not necessary to list here, served to emphasise his divine powers and to differentiate him from other spirit-mediums.

The successful medium, then, relies on his capacity as a diviner, his ability to foster a wide circle of adherents, his ability as a showman, and a certain amount of luck. David/*Kafudzi*'s phenomenal rise was exceptional in its scale and rapidity, but it was also normal. Spirit-mediums rise and fall in popularity and their success or failure in capturing and manipulating public opinion affects not only the relative standing of the mediums themselves, but also that of the spirits which they present. David/*Kafudzi*'s position is therefore precarious. As we shall see later, not all the people of Chiota believed in his powers and even those who do may one day become disillusioned. Should this occur, they may easily bring about his downfall. Spirit-mediums are continuously subject to being discredited and it is to the mechanisms of discrediting that we now turn.

The possibility of fraud

The people of Chiota are no more credulous that any other people and mediums may easily be discredited.[10] Evans-Pritchard (1937 : 183) observed with surprise that the Azande are especially sceptical of their witch-doctors. He further noted that such scepticism was as much an institutionalised part of Zande life as was faith.

It is important to note that scepticism about witch-doctors is not socially repressed. Absence of formal and coercive doctrines permit Azande to state that many, even most, witch-doctors are frauds. No opposition being offered to such statements they leave the main belief in the prophetic and therapeutic powers of witch-doctors unimpaired. Indeed, scepticism is included in the pattern of belief in witch-doctors. Faith and scepticism are alike traditional. Scepticism explains failures of witch-doctors, and being directed towards particular witch-doctors even tends to support faith in others. (1937 : 193)

The Zezuru of Chiota have a similar attitude to their spirit-mediums; they believe and they doubt, and just as there exist mechanisms which permit the rise to fame of successful mediums, there exist others which act as restraints on the over ambitious. Mediums may be discredited either totally, partially or situationally.

A medium may be said to be totally discredited when no-one continues to believe in his mediumship. Such total falls from grace are rare, but during fieldwork I noted one case. This medium had experienced a rise to fame similar to that of David/*Kafudzi* and such was the size of his clientelle that he was able to construct a large and impressive seance house which was visited by clients from Chiota and beyond. In a short space of time, however, his reputation crumbled; the seance house became empty and the discredited medium was obliged to leave Chiota to earn his living selling herbs and charms in the African townships of Salisbury. I was able to discover two reasons for this medium's demise although there may have been others. The first was that he was accused of having committed incest with his brother's daughter, his own classificatory daughter. His brother had come to consult him about his chances of becoming chief. The medium, in trance, explained to him that his chances would be improved if he were to have sexual relations with his (the medium's) daughter while he (the medium) had sexual relations with his daughter. The case came to light after the medium's classificatory daughter became pregnant and gave birth. During childbirth she confessed to having slept with her father's brother.[11] The publicity which surrounded this scandal was great and the guilty parties, the medium and his brother, were obliged to pay compensation of eight head of cattle which were ritually slaughtered and eaten at the chief's village. The second reason given for the medium's disgrace was that he had become so ambitious as to claim the mediumship of the spirit of Adam. In order to draw attention to the veracity of his claim the medium danced naked in trance.

After these two accusations had acquired common currency, the medium was totally discredited to the extent that his status as spirit-medium was removed from him, and he was re-classified as a fraud.

More common than total discrediting is the practice of partial discrediting. This occurs when a group of persons challenges the identity of the medium's spirit-presentation without challenging his *mediumship*. In the extended case presented in chapter 5 a medium claims to be possessed by a hero spirit; while one faction supports his claim another believes him to be possessed by an aggrieved ancestor spirit (*ngozi*). In this and other similar cases, it is important to note that there is generally disagreement between sectors of the population as to the supposed identity of the spirit presented.

In October 1963, *Drum* magazine published an article about a medium whom they called the 'Wild Man',[12] who lived near Chiota at a place called Chitungwiza and who claimed to be the medium of *Chaminuka*. The last recorded medium of this legendary Pan Shona spirit is believed to have died at Chitungwiza after having been captured by the Mandebele during their strife with the Shona in the nineteenth century.[13]

Soon after this publication the *Drum* offices were visited by one Muchatera who himself claimed to be the true *Chaminuka* medium. He observed that it was impossible for two mediums to act as host for the same spirit.[14] Muchatera lived near Rusape and had already appeared in Gelfand's *Shona Ritual* (1959) as the medium of *Chaminuka*.[15] *Drum* therefore arranged for the two mediums to meet at Chitungwiza. The meeting was reported as having been dramatic. The 'Wild Man' took the offensive and, dressed only in a leopard skin, denounced Muchatera for wearing a suit, tie and shoes, and for having travelled by car. Muchatera, for his part, reacted by making deprecatory comments about the 'Wild Man's' maize crop which was singularly dry considering that it was growing in the gardens of a famous prophet and rain-maker. According to *Drum*, the 'Wild Man' accepted the challenge, climbed up a small rock, waved his arms and rain clouds appeared.

The meeting ended soon after this when the 'Wild Man' and his followers demanded the withdrawal of Muchatera who was obliged to leave to the derision of the 'Wild Man' and his followers. Later the 'Wild Man' announced that Muchatera was not the medium of *Chaminuka*, but of *Zhanje*, a *mbira* player of a previous *Chaminuka* medium.

The import of the *Drum* article was that the 'Wild Man' was the true *Chaminuka* medium whereas Muchatera was a fraud. However, such questions are relative, for the status of a particular medium depends on the population which supports him. In this case, Muchatera's authority was based on his followers who were far away in Rusape. The 'Wild Man's' status as the true medium of *Chaminuka* was guaranteed by the presence of his followers at Chitungwiza. Muchatera was partially discredited because he was 'playing away' and it is quite probable that the outcome would have been reversed had the meeting taken place in Rusape.

The final and least radical mode of discrediting spirit-mediums I call situational because it involves only a temporary questioning of a spirit-medium's legitimacy. It is the most common occurrence and involves the medium being suspected of feigning trance for one reason or another. Such accusations, although they may affect the long-term credibility of the medium involved, challenge neither the medium's credentials as spirit-medium nor the identity of the spirit presented.

With all these possibilities for discrediting mediums, it is clear that they are severely constrained in their words and deeds by public opinion. But how could it be otherwise? Their only sanctions are mystical ones and these can only be effective as long as people are prepared to believe in them.

Spirit-mediums are judged to be good or bad, true or false, not so much on their performance at their initiation rituals, nor by the backing that they might achieve from other better-established mediums, but by their day-to-day performance.

Having discussed ways in which mediums may rise and fall from grace we are now in a position to take another look at the total system.

The system as a whole

The people of Chiota think of their religious organisation in the same way as their political organisation. When describing the relationships between spirit-mediums they draw the parallel with the political structure, noting that just as the village headman refers unsolved cases to his subchief who in his turn refers them to the chief, so the junior ancestors give way to more senior ones, who in their turn recognise the superiority of the heroes. However, in practice, neither the lay public nor the mediums recognise such a cut-and-dried ordering of ritual authority; the system is much more fluid than the ideal would have it. Although the system is *thought of* in stable hierarchical terms, and although there is a certain stability of authority relations between spirit-mediums, the pattern of relationships between the spirits and their mediums at any one point of time depends more on the abilities of the mediums than on anything else. Even in the case of those low-level mediums who act as hosts for junior ancestor spirits whose genealogical relationships with one another are not disputed, there is no guarantee that the same relationships will be observed between their *mediums* and it is quite common to find dissention within lineages about the relative merits of certain spirits and their mediums.

The overall situation is best described in terms of networks and spheres of influence. Each medium, on being initiated, incorporates himself into the ritual network of the mediums who are involved in the initiation. If he is successful as a high-level medium he in his turn will initiate new mediums who join the wider network through joining his, and so on. In this way successful mediums are able to build up networks which ramify continuously and which are not bounded. These spheres of influence reach the lay public through their contact with the mediums as clients and as attenders of rituals, but these ritual networks are not stable or exclusive. Their stability is threatened by the competition between mediums which is endemic to the system and which may bring a medium to challenge the authority of the medium who initiated him, in order to alter relationships within the network or to establish a new network with him as centre. Exclusivity is prejudiced because people are not obliged to swear allegiance to any one medium. Sick people may consult any number of mediums before finding a satisfactory answer to their problems, and mediums at the start of their careers tend often to seek the ritual support of more than one high-level medium/sponsor.

Because of this lack of stability or exclusiveness, the total ritual network, composed of the partial networks which grow up about each medium, is a complex web of social relationships which bears little relation to the tidy hierarchy by which the system is *thought of* by the people of Chiota and which has been described for other Shona groups in Rhodesia hithertofore.[16] Because the pattern of relationships between mediums and their spirits and the lay public are constantly changing due to the constant rise and fall in popularity of mediums, any analytical model which may be derived to account for the system must itself be dynamic, and capable of accounting for the essentially charismatic nature of spirit-mediums' authority.

Charisma and its control

Weber (1968 : 48) defined charisma as 'a certain quality of an individual personality by virtue of which he is set apart from ordinary men and treated as endowed with supernatural, superhuman or at least exceptional powers or qualities'. Even though Worsley (1968) was right to criticise Weber for overemphasising the personal aspect of charisma and for playing down the significance of the social context in which charismatic authority is exercised, Weber was quite clearly aware of the fact that this type of authority was only effective if the holder of charisma

45

was able to maintain the loyalty of his following by satisfying their expectations.

> Charisma knows only inner determination and inner restraint. The holder of charisma seizes the task that is adequate for him and demands obedience and a following by virtue of his mission. His success determines whether he finds them. His charismatic claim breaks down if his mission is not recognised by those to whom he feels he has been sent. If they recognise him, he is their master — so long as he knows how to maintain recognition through 'proving' himself. (Weber 1968 : 20)

> If proof of his charismatic qualification fails him for long, the leader endowed with charisma tends to think his god or his magical or heroic powers have deserted him. If he is for long unsuccessful, above all if his leadership fails to benefit his followers, it is likely that his charismatic authority will disappear. This is the genuine charismatic meaning of the 'gift of grace'. (Weber 1968 : 49—50)

Thus Weber did not conceive of charisma as a purely individual phenomenon but as a social fact. Charismatic authority exists only as long as the individual concerned succeeds in 'benefiting' his followers; as long as his words and deeds are somehow relevant in the social context in which he finds himself. In this sense Zezuru mediums are charismatic figures. The ease with which mediums may be discredited or boosted in status indicates that it is society which credits them with their super-human powers only as long as it requires, for one reason or another, to believe in them. Their claim to mediumship breaks down if the medium does not continue to be recognised by those to whom he feels he has been sent.

How can the concept of charisma lead to an understanding of Zezuru religious organisation in Chiota? David represents a case of almost 'pure' charisma in Weber's terms. The corporate group which formed around him was 'based on an emotional form of communal relationship' (Weber 1968 : 50), and the social relationships developed were 'strictly personal, based on the validity and practice of charismatic personal qualities' (Weber 1968 : 54). His success in establishing these relationships of dependence was measured by the seniority of his possessing spirit so that it is possible to regard *Kafudzi* the hero as a reification of David Mudiwa's charismatic authority.

However, even David exploited an existing institutional framework for the realisation of his charismatic qualities, and even if his nationalistic message and his ritual techniques were important innovations, he was working within generally established procedures. Other spirit-mediums act as hosts for already well-established hero and ancestor spirits and although their individual efforts may bring about changes in the relative standing of them, basically what they are doing is occupying traditionally hallowed offices, however vaguely defined.

In other words, the religious organisation of Chiota has to be understood not as a free for all charismatic contest, but as a continual process of charismatic modification and its subsequent routinisation. Looked at in this light, the well-established hero spirits like *Chaminuka, Nehanda, Chitswachegore*, etc. are the objective manifestations of the charisma of their early mediums. Through many generations of being represented by competent mediums their status as heroes has become invulnerable, even if their standing, relative to one another, depends on the charismatic qualities of their respective mediums.

There is no conclusive evidence to show that this is, in fact, what happens; a process which takes some four generations to complete itself cannot be observed in two years' fieldwork; but this dynamic model does make sense of the facts and, as Gellner (1969 : 158) has so wisely remarked, 'A model which assumes stability over time is just as speculative as one which postulates change.' It is even possible to suggest that *Chaminuka* and *Nehanda* began their careers as hero spirits through mediums like David Mudiwa and Kagubi (see below, p. 48) who were in their time regarded as upstarts by those mediums who felt that their authority was being threatened. Similarly it could be conjectured that *Kafudzi* might continue to be presented by mediums after David Mudiwa's death until he also enters the ranks of the fully established hero spirits. Weber (1968 : 54) noted that 'in its pure form charismatic authority may be said to exist only in the process of originating. It cannot remain stable, but becomes either tradition-alised or rationalised, or a combination of both', and even after only three years of operations, the group of people which had gathered around David/*Kafudzi* was beginning to show signs of bureaucratisation. Those who committed them-selves to a total dedication to David/*Kafudzi* and his works had become suf-ficiently dependent on him to have developed their own keen interest in the permanence of the venture. Because such interests 'become conspicuously evi-dent with the disappearance of the personal charismatic leader and with the problem of succession' (Weber 1968 : 55), it is reasonable to assume that when David Mudiwa dies, his administrative staff will ensure that the person who is recognised as the new medium of *Kafudzi*, as the successor to David Mudiwa's charisma, will be capable of continuing the tradition. Thus will *Kafudzi* be guaranteed permanence and stability as a hero spirit on a par with *Chaminuka* and *Nehanda*.[17]

Having analysed the way in which spirit-mediums build up their prestige in the community and how they relate to one another and to the lay public through networks of relationships, spheres of influence which are a measure of pure and routinised charisma, it now remains to examine the situations in which spirit-mediums to beyond their roles as diviners, healers and rain-makers to turn their hard-won reputations to political action.[18]

Spirit-mediums as leaders

For the most part the spirit-mediums of Chiota do not emerge as political *leaders* although their activities as diviners of misfortune inevitably lead them to make political *decisions*. Because it is believed that misfortune is brought about by up-sets in social relations, any explanation of misfortune is also a political statement.

47

High-level mediums help villagers make decisions, but they do not generally lead political factions. Low-level mediums are so preoccupied with maintaining some semblance of consensus in their villages and lineages that they tend to refer contentious issues to 'outsider' high-level mediums or *ngangas*.

However, in at least one historical situation, the Shona Rebellion of 1896—7, the spirit-mediums of Central Mashonaland led and co-ordinated a widespread political revolt; and on various occasions at lower levels of social structure, spirit mediums did and do emerge as leaders. The same sociological principles operate with differences largely of scale at all levels of social structure.

Low-level mediums in village politics

In localised lineage groups one member of the lineage is usually regarded as the senior spirit-medium and he is consulted about all matters of lineage importance. They tend to avoid contentious issues but are sometimes forced out of their neutrality when consensus breaks down and when differences of opinion are so serious as to jeopardise the continuing solidarity of the lineage. In these circumstances the rival faction within the lineage may challenge the overall authority of the original senior-spirit medium and produce one from their own ranks as an alternative. When this happens opposing groups may concentrate their political opposition around the ritual competition between their respective mediums, who take on the mantle of faction leadership. In the extended case which is analysed in chapter 5 it will be shown how in one village two mediums came to be the *foci* for the conflicting aims of two political factions whose action, with respect to one another, was largely 'dictated' by them. Protest was channeled through the voice of the spirits who converted *vox populi* into *vox dei* so that the lineage finally split up ostensibly on the orders of one of the spirit-mediums in trance.

In such situations, low-level spirit mediums co-ordinate grievances, give them sacred authority and catalyse political action.

High-level mediums and the rebellion

In 1896 a number of Shona groups in Central Mashonaland broke out in bloody rebellion against the white settlers who had installed themselves in the region following Cecil Rhodes' Pioneer Column in 1890. Ranger (1967), in his remarkable analysis of the rebellion shows how certain important spirit-mediums co-ordinated and led the rebellion, by giving sacred authority to the widespread grievances of the Shona people and by providing an organisational framework which was capable of uniting otherwise politically independent chiefdoms.

The supreme leader of the rebellion was the medium Gumboreshumba/*Kagubi*, whose rise to fame from being the medium of a 'common or barn door Mondoro' to the medium of *Murenga*, the Son of God, bears striking resemblance to that of

48

David/*Kafudzi*. Ranger admits the possibility that Gumboreshumba/*Kagubi* was, in fact, an established spirit-medium before the rebellion, but favours the interpretation that 'the Kagubi medium's commanding influence developed only in association with the movement towards rebellion' (Ranger 1967 : 215).

The Rhodesian Native Department, writes Ranger (1967 : 215), 'were decisive in the view that the Kagubi medium had not been an important figure before the rising; and equally decisive in their view that during it he had been by far the most important figure'. Native Commissioner Cambell described the medium of *Kagubi* as follows: 'Kagubi was of no more importance than any other common or barn door Mondoro . . . He was only a common Mondoro, scores of which can be found in every district.' (Ranger 1967 : 215). The Chief Native Commissioner contrasted the status of *Kagubi* as a newcomer with that of the well-established medium of *Nehanda*, who was 'by far the most important wizard in Mashonaland and was in the habit of receiving tribute from all the chiefs who took part in the rebellion' (Ranger 1967 : 215). However, as Ranger observes, the Chief Native Commissioner was obliged to recognise the fact that the medium of *Nehanda*, in spite of her customary seniority, sent tribute to the *Kagubi* medium. In a relatively short period of time, therefore, *Kagubi* rose to supercede the traditionally hallowed *Nehanda*.

Ranger shows how the *Kagubi* medium was strategically related to certain key chiefs and was able to act as a link between the co-ordinators of the rebellion amongst the Ndebele and the discontented people of Mashonaland. As time went on *Kagubi* began to be known as *Murenga* which became almost synonymous with the rebellion itself and which some claim to have meant Son of God. Gumboreshumba's change of spirit name could be interpreted in much the same way as we have interpreted *Kafudzi*'s transformation from water spirit to hero.

Gumboreshumba/*Kagubi*/*Murenga* continued to direct much of the strategy of the rebellion and to co-ordinate the activities of the autonomous chiefs through his spirit-medium network; he and the *Nehanda* medium became the main targets of the white offensive once their crucial role had been understood. White troops, however, had great difficulty in running them to ground and it was only in October of 1897 that Gumboreshumba was taken into custody after the surrender of such important chiefs as Kunzwi-Nyandoro and Mashiangombe. In December of 1897 the medium of *Nehanda* was captured. They were both sentenced to death and were hanged on 27 April 1898. *Nehanda* went to the scaffold refusing baptism but Gumboreshumba was baptised into the Catholic faith shortly before his death.

The significance of the leadership of Gumboreshumba lies in the fact that he did not belong to any pre-established hierarchy of spirits and spirit-mediums. The rebellion could not, therefore, be understood in terms of a pre-existing organisation. Ranger concludes that the Shona religious system was flexible enough to allow for such sporadic eruptions which occurred in response to changing political and economic conditions. His data led him to perceive that the Shona religious system could not be understood in terms of stable hierarchies of ritual authority as most of the ethnography suggested.

We have so far written of the involvement of these systems [the religious systems of the Shona and Ndebele] as the involvement of 'traditional' religious officers and structures: an elaborate and aged machinery lying to hand which was made use of in the rebellion of 1896. Such a view has a certain truth but we should not forget two things. One is that the systems as they existed in 1896 were the products of countless changes, some of which have already been indicated; they were not static or fixed, nor were the relationships between the various priests and mediums. The other is that however much these systems were linked up with supratribal or tribal political systems – with the institutional 'establishments' of Shona history – they still retained their essential charismatic character. From out of the Mwari cult and from out of the hierarchies of the spirit mediums there could emerge – and no doubt there often had in the past emerged – charismatic prophet figures, whose spiritual power or power of personality was capable of throwing relationships within the cults into a new pattern, and who were able to break away from the established inter-relationship with political authority. One might speculate indeed that a constant theme of Shona political history has been the rise and fall of figures of this kind, sometimes offering a challenge to established political power, sometimes acting as a rallying point in a period of political breakdown, as the great Chaminuka mediums did in the middle decades of the nineteenth century. (Ranger 1967 : 213)

But Ranger is not satisfied with portraying Gumboreshumba/*Kagubi* simply as an articulator of grievance. He gave to these grievances direction and purpose.

It is clear that the Kagubi medium not only played a very important role in co-ordinating the rising at a supra-tribal level, but also that as the prophetic leader of a revolutionary rebellion he exercised a much more authoritarian command than anthropologists have found to be the case with spirit mediums in 'normal' situations. The spirit medium is said to be an expresser of the consensus rather than a commander; but though the Kagubi medium could also be described as the articulator of the consensus that the time had come to rebel he was clearly more than that. After the rising had broken out he continued to plan an authoritarian role. He not only stimulated the first killings but also in some sense directed them, making sure that goods taken from the whites were sent to him and taking particular care over the distribution of firearms. (Ranger 1967 : 223–4)

Ranger is, I think, quite right to perceive that the mediums in the rebellion were 'more authoritarian' than they are in 'normal' times. Even in cases of village fission, the mediums do more than simply give voice to common consensus; they achieve a political leadership which goes beyond their function as personalised public opinion polls. Why is this so?

Ranger gives the clue in the following observation. 'The Kagubi medium was more than a senior spirit medium. *He brought thousands of Shona into membership of a new society*, the true believers in the M'lenga, with their own distinguishing symbols and obligations and their own promises of divine favour.' (Ranger 1967 : 225, my italics.)

The sociology of spirit-mediumship

Emile Durkheim talked about two kinds of society. One was homogeneous and simple and based on what he called mechanical solidarity. The other was heterogeneous, characterised by a division of labour and whose solidarity he termed organic. Societies with a minimal division of labour, according to Durkheim, derive their solidarity from their very homogeneity; they are marked by a strong *conscience collective*, which, in the case of the simplest societies, where there was perfect homogeneity and perfect consensus, would be given objective reality as the god of that society. Durkheim believed that Australian aboriginal clans closely approximated to this kind of society and used them as empirical evidence for his hypothesis. The totem, he notes,

expressed and symbolises two different sorts of things. In the first place, it is the outward and visible form of what we have called the totemic principle or god. But it is also the symbol of the determined society called the clan. It is its flag; it is the sign by which each clan distinguishes itself from the others, the visible mark of its personality, a mark borne by everything which is a part of the clan under any title whatsoever, men, beasts or things. So if it is at once the symbol of the god and of the society, is that not because the god and the society are only one? (Durkheim 1961 : 236)

Although Durkheim did not turn his attention to situations of conflict, he did perceive that what he understood as 'society' was not necessarily a social system hallowed by time and tradition with a stable social structure; he was therefore able to extend the insights he had drawn from the totemic Australian clans to such apparently distant phenomena as the Crusades and the French Revolution.

This aptitude of society for setting itself up as a god or for creating gods was never more apparent than during the first years of the French Revolution. At this time, in fact, under the influence of the general enthusiasm, things purely laical by nature were transformed by public opinion into sacred things: these were the Fatherland, Liberty, Reason. It is true that this religious renovation had only an ephemeral duration. But that was because the patriotic enthusiasm which at first transported the masses soon relaxed. The cause being gone, the effect could not remain. But this experiment, though short-lived, keeps all its sociological interest. It remains true that in one determined case we have seen society and its essential ideas become, directly and with no transfiguration of any sort, the object of a veritable cult. (Durkheim 1961 : 245)

Ranger noted that the Shona mediums brought about a *new* society, as indeed all true charismatic leaders do. But what kind of a society? According to Max Weber (1968 : 50),

The corporate group which is subject to charismatic authority is based on an emotional norm of communal relationship. The administrative staff of a charismatic leader does not consist of 'officials'; at least its members are not technically trained. It is not chosen on the basis of social privilege nor from the point of view of domestic or personal dependency. There is no hierarchy. There is no such thing as a definite sphere of authority and of competence, and no appropriation of official powers on the basis of social privileges.

51

Here Weber is surely describing the type of society of which Durkheim would have attributed mechanical solidarity. The leader's followers exist as a society because they have one thing, and one thing only in common, which is the leader and his message. They do not exist as a society without him, nor he without them.

Once seen in this light, it is tempting to suggest that the charismatic leader is the materialisation of the *conscience collective* of the society which he brings into being. In this case the leader of this type is sacred not by definition, but as a consequence of his symbolic status. It is interesting that (at least in English translation) both Weber, in defining charisma, and Durkheim, in defining the sacred, use the same words. 'The term "charisma" ', says Weber (1968 : 48), 'will be applied to a certain quality of an individual personality by virtue of which *he is set apart from* ordinary men . . . ' (my italics). Durkheim defines religion as, 'a unified system of beliefs and practices relative to sacred things, that is to say, *things set apart and forbidden* . . . ' I suggest that the charisma of personal leaders is an attribution of the society that they originate and a recognition of the total inter-dependence between one and the other. Such leaders exist and are seen as sacred because they are seen as (and indeed are) the very *raison d'être* of the society of followers that they lead.

But this does not yet explain why charismatic leaders in general and Shona spirit-mediums in particular should appear as authoritarian figures. Perhaps the answer lies in the frequent assertion that charismatic leaders act as catalysts of social action.

Charismatic leaders are catalysts in the sense that they spark off a reaction which transforms what had previously been a mere agglomerate of individuals into a society. They transform a situation in which a number of individuals happen to have certain individual representations in common into one where these same individuals share them as collective representation. The Shona mediums of 1896 were able to give dramatic reality to a number of widespread, yet individually held, grievances and by taking them out of the private domain into the public, to create a new society with these grievances transformed into a *conscience collective*. It was surely this act of catalysis that enabled them to unleash passions and actions which would be out of the question without the necessary consciousness of solidarity. Durkheim (1961 : 241–2) pointed out in relation to crowd psychology that 'under the influence of the general exaltation, we see the most mediocre and inoffensive bourgeois become either a hero or a butcher'.

By trying to see the link between Weber's analysis of charisma and Durkheim's basic principles of the sociology of consensus, I have tried to describe the processes by which charismatic leaders are seen as sacred and 'set apart from ordinary men' and to show how, as the mouthpieces of public opinion, they derive their authority. As Durkheim (1961 : 238–9) questioned, 'so opinion, primarily a social thing, is a source of authority, and it might even be asked whether all authority is not the daughter of opinion'. But I do not claim to have reduced the magic of charisma to a sociological explanation. In the first place, it must not be assumed that it is easy to know what public opinion is, even in a society as small as Chiota Tribal Trust Land, and even if the only task of a spirit-medium were to regurgitate common consensus, it would defy the efforts of most men. But when it comes to the *effective* voicing of public opinion, at the right time, in the right place and in the right way, sociological analysis ends. Even after one has analysed the techniques employed by David Mudiwa and searched out the minutest details of Kagubi's career, one is still far short of the mark. They are both great men, and, in spite of the fact that the roots of their authority lay in what was already there, latent in society, they created something new. Charismatic leaders in general, and Zezuru spirit-mediums in particular build on the past and the present, but their conservatism ends there.

4
Zezuru flexibility and Korekore rigidity

The dynamic model proposed to take account of the operation of the spirit-mediums of Chiota Tribal Trust Land was felt necessary in order to make sense of a very complex reality. The general picture is of a vital religious organisation against the background of a dynamically changing social situation. To a considerable extent the flexibility and uncertainty of the 'traditional' religion of Chiota mirror similar characteristics in the mundane sphere of politics and economics. As was shown in chapter 1 Chiota's close proximity to Salisbury means that the people of Chiota are the first to be affected by the political and economic upheavals so much a characteristic of Southern Rhodesia in the last 15 years.

The Korekore of Mount Darwin District are much further removed from these upheavals, and Garbett has shown that their system of spirit-mediumship is much more tightly controlled than that of the Zezuru and that hierarchies of spirits and mediums really exist. In view of this marked difference between the religious organisation of two Shona-speaking peoples it is as well to embark on the task of comparative analysis of Shona institutions.

The Korekore

The Korekore are organised into small chiefdoms in the Zambesi Valley, successors of the once great Munhumutapa Kingdom (Korekore 'royals' claim patrilineal descent from Mutota, whom Abraham (1959 : 59–84) has identified with Munhumutapa.) Korekore chiefdoms, therefore, have an historical unity.

Korekore chiefdoms are loosely structured around these royal lineages. They are composed of small hamlets which are short lived and prone to fission. Areas are vast and the population density varies between 6 and 8 persons per square mile. Supra-chiefdom relations are comparatively complex, but are confined to the cult of the spirit mediums.

Garbett (1969 : 105) notes that although spirit-possession, in Firth's terms (see above p. 30) is very common among the Korekore, spirit-*mediumship* is 'comparatively rare'. Furthermore, there are no mediums of the recently dead ancestors, as among the Zezuru. Mediumship of these ancestors is confined to those people (mostly women) 'who act as mediums for malevolent ancestor spirits (*ngozi*) believed grossly offended by some misdemeanour of their living descendants'.[1] Rather, most Korekore mediums are possessed by 'the voices of long-dead spirits whose influence is now manifested among the living by their

54

supposed control over the rainfall and fertility of particular pieces of land' (Garbett 1969 : 105).

These senior spirits represent the uppermost generations of the fifteen generation deep Korekore genealogy. This part of the genealogy serves as a charter in the Malinowskian sense for the relationships between the various mediums and also for the status of its agnatic descendants as 'true Korekore', members of ruling lineages. Relationships in this part of the genealogy appear to be stable, for descent from any ancestor at this level serves only to distinguish royal Korekore from commoner Korekore.

Garbett (1969 : 106) notes that 'Korekore mediums do not mediate just any spirit haphazard. They are organized into a system . . .', and that there are two aspects to this system, one territorial, the other lineal.

The land in which the Korekore live is divided up into what Garbett (1969 : 107) calls 'spirit-provinces', each 'named after, and associated with, the spirit of a man who is thought to have been one of the original Karanga invaders,[2] a descendant of an invader, or, less commonly, an autochthon'. The spirits of these men, who are usually believed to have been the first occupiers of their 'spirit-provinces', are reckoned to control rainfall and fertility within their provinces. Garbett (1969 : 107) calls these men 'spirit-guardians' and shows how 'the spirit-provinces are articulated into a single system, which I term a spirit-realm, by a long genealogy which shows the relations among spirit-guardians. In the case of Mutota's spirit-realm the genealogy is some 15 generations in depth.' Thus, in Mutota's spirit-realm, there is a distinct hierarchy of spirit-guardians which is expressed in putative genealogical relationships between the spirit-guardians. This hierarchy is significant with regard to rainfall, for if the rain rituals fail in one spirit-province, representations are made up the hierarchy until finally Mutota is reached, being the apex, and ultimate authority. Garbett (1969 : 110) notes that this territorial hierarchy is stable and that 'mystical sanctions appear to operate to discourage a medium with territorial ambitions from usurping another's territory'.

Spirit-provinces are not congruent with chiefdoms and on matters of rain and the fertility of the earth men consult the medium of the spirit-guardian of the spirit-province in which they live.

The 'territorial hierarchy' is also a 'genealogical hierarchy'. 'Unlike the territorial aspect of spirit-mediumship which involves people because they happen to be living on a particular piece of land which falls in the province of a particular spirit-guardian, the lineal aspect involves people who are members of widely dispersed agnatic descent groups believed to have been founded by certain spirit-guardians.' (Garbett 1969 : 112). The problems for which this lineal hierarchy is usually invoked are those related to the inheritance of wives and property, succession to family titles, deaths and sicknesses attributed to the malevolence of ancestral spirits. In addition mediums are significant in situations of succession to chiefship. 'In the lineal aspect of the system the total hierarchy of mediums

55

may be utilised, for should people not get satisfaction from one medium they go to another more senior in the hierarchy and so on until the senior medium is reached.' (Garbett 1969 : 112) Indeed it is only in the person of Mutota that the lineal and territorial aspects of the system merge, since he is the apex of both hierarchies.

Entrance and acceptance into the status of spirit-mediumship among the Korekore is controlled by extremely rigorous procedures. Garbett (1969 : 116) describes how Korekore neophyte mediums must go through tests lasting a number of years during which they progress up the hierarchy of mediums, the tests getting increasingly severe. 'The tests conducted by the senior spirit-mediums may be very searching. The candidate is supposed to fall possessed in the presence of the senior medium and the possessing spirit-guardian should answer questions about his (i.e. the spirit-guardian's) past life, the site of his grave, the boundaries of his spirit-province, and, most importantly, the genealogy which connects him to the possessing spirit of the senior medium. As a final test the candidate has to select, from a number of such objects kept by the senior medium, the ritual staff used by the previous medium of the spirit-guardian concerned.' As could be expected, many candidates fail the tests, being told that they are possessed only by a *shave*. Garbett (1969 : 116) adds: 'Persons who just arrive and announce that they are possessed by a particular spirit are unlikely to be accepted. It is only those mediums who are sponsored by important mediums in the system, and who have successfully passed the preliminary tests, who appear to stand any chance of acceptance. Thus recruitment to the system is controlled by the senior spirit-medium in conjunction with the other mediums.'

Occasionally new spirit-mediums emerge claiming to be possessed by 'new spirits' – i.e. those who have not previously been presented by mediums. These new spirit-guardians are absorbed into the existing lineal hierarchy according to their genealogical status and into the territorial hierarchy by being allotted a sub-division of an existing spirit-province.

One of the consequences of this rigid hierarchial system, maintained by rigorous selection procedures is that mediums, once allotted a position in the hierarchy, are given a specific area of jurisdiction which they cannot exceed. There would appear to be no opportunity for mediums to improve their status once installed.

With the important caveat that Korekore mediums do not achieve advancement with age, the Korekore religious organisation can be seen to conform quite closely to Weber's ideal of a bureaucratic structure. Taking spirit guardians as the offices of this bureaucracy, the main bureaucratic features of the Korekore system are as follows:

(1)   The existence of a hierarchy of offices with 'levels of graded authority' in a 'firmly ordered system of super- and sub-ordination in which there is a supervision of the lower offices by the higher ones' (Weber 1946 : 197).

(2)   The marked separation of incumbent and office. Garbett notes that in

56

general, spirit-mediums are treated by Korekore as ordinary members of society unless they are actually in trance, in which state they completely lose their own personalities, taking over those of their spirit-guardians. When the incumbent moves into his office – i.e. when he moves into trance – he becomes so much a part of his office that when he comes out of it he is unaware of what he has done in it. This important principle (which is also a feature of the Zezuru system) is also evident in the clear distinction which is supposed to be maintained between the incomes which accrue to a spirit-medium in his capacities as a person and a spirit. The income which is earned by the spirit must be used for the spirit's business for example feeding clients, building seance houses, buying ritual paraphernalia etc. but not for the personal consumption of the medium and his friends and family. If such behaviour is suspected it might lead to the discrediting of a medium. The 'office' income is kept separate from that of the incumbent.

(3)   Weber maintains that office holders in a bureaucracy must undergo 'expert training', and Garbett (1969 : 117) has shown that Korekore neophyte mediums must train if they are to be accepted as mediums. 'Close investigation of the backgrounds of a number of mediums revealed that all appeared to have had long periods of direct association with other mediums prior to their possession. Subsequently they had further periods of contact either with the same mediums, or with others during the preliminary tests of the probationary period. It is during these periods both prior and subsequent to possession that mediums appear to acquire the skills and esoteric knowledge which enable them to become established mediums.' During this period mediums in training 'acquire the esoteric knowledge of traditional history and genealogies which is so important for their acceptance and for the maintenance of their position'. In this way, then, the identity of offices is maintained, successive office holders fulfilling their proper and expected roles.

(4)   As in Weber's ideal bureaucratic structure, the office holders in the Korekore spirit-medium organisation are appointed by senior authority. It is from senior members in the hierarchy that a Korekore medium derives his legitimacy as the medium of his guardian spirit, for it is they who decide on his genuineness or otherwise. They, the senior mediums, are the holders of this responsibility on behalf of Korekore society.

Thus, Korekore mediums derive their legitimacy not so much from their achievement of a following – i.e. 'from below' – but from more senior mediums – i.e. 'from above'. Those over whom they exercise their authority do not choose their mediums. They are chosen for them. A medium's following is not defined by his own personal qualities so much as by the areas of jurisdiction (defined in territorial and genealogical terms) assigned by tradition to his spirit-guardian.

Korekore and Zezuru

The Korekore religious system is, then, considerably more rigid than that of the

57

Spirits of protest

Zezuru of Chiota. The salient differences are presented in table 2, and elaborated one by one.

Table 2

	Korekore	Zezuru
Spirits presented	The 'long dead' over five generations from living	Continuous, ranging from the most recent dead through to the heroes and founders of clans
Structure	Hierarchy, rigid and stable through time	No hierarchy, highly fluid
Legitimisation procedure	Through tests administered by more senior mediums	Recognition of established mediums a necessary but not sufficient condition of legitimacy, which is finally conferred by 'belief' of following
Basis of authority	'From above' (i.e. senior mediums), 'bureaucratic'	'From below' (i.e. consensus of lay public), 'charismatic'
Mobility	Only downwards when discredited	Both upwards and downwards
Rivalry	Highly circumscribed	Endemic

Spirits presented

Spirit-mediumship amongst the Korekore is confined to the long dead. However, among the Zezuru, as we have already shown, all spirits ranging from the most junior *mudzimu* to the most senior *gombwe* may talk through mediums. Korekore mediums, therefore, are to be compared, in the main, with the high-level mediums of Chiota.

It must be noted, however, that Korekore spirits define not only the status of their mediums, but also the relative status of their agnatic descendants. Among the Zezuru of Chiota, this is only true of the recently dead ancestors. Very senior ancestors and hero spirits do not articulate social groups or define the status of their descendants. Furthermore, whereas Korekore spirit guardians are all descended from Mutota, Zezuru spirits are heterogeneous and have no common ancestor. Descent from Mutota makes a Korekore a 'true Korekore'. There are no 'true Zezuru', in this sense, there being no such aristocratic clan.

58

Zezuru flexibility and Korekore rigidity

Structure

The rigidity of the Korekore hierarchy of spirit-guardian contrasts sharply with the Chiota situation where there is no hierarchy of spirits. Professional mediums build up 'spheres of influence' which fluctuate in size over time as mediums rise and fall in popularity. The imputed seniority of any spirit is related to the relative popularity of its medium. Furthermore there is no general consensus throughout Chiota of the relative standing of mediums at any particular time. Supporters of one medium will affirm the superior status of his possessing spirit to the detriment of another rival medium and vice versa.

Even at the level of the mediums of junior ancestors, where genealogical status is open to less dispute, mediums of more senior spirits cannot count on the support of all the lineal descendants of that spirit, who may align themselves behind the medium of a more junior spirit. Even at this level, then, there is considerable flexibility.

Legitimation procedure

Whereas amongst the Korekore the recognition of senior mediums would appear to be a necessary *and* sufficient condition for the establishment of a new medium, this is not the case for Chiota mediums. In Chiota, where there is no overall agreement as to the relative status of the various professional mediums, the new would-be medium is in a predicament, for he may acquire the backing of one medium only to find that this is worthless beyond the sphere of influence of that medium.

Authority of mediums

This is closely related to the above point. Whereas Korekore mediums receive their authority from 'above', from more senior mediums, the mediums of Chiota derive their authority from the recognition accorded them by other mediums and the lay public, 'from below'. They are charismatic figures.

Rivalry

The constraints imposed on rivalry between Korekore mediums are absent in Chiota. Indeed, rivalry is endemic in the Chiota system, where mediums compete with one another for clients and recognition. We have seen how this is the case for mediums at village level as well as at the level of the professional mediums where mechanisms such as exist among the Korekore for restraining rivalry are absent. For example, David/*Kafudzi* was to hold an important ritual; he sent a messenger to invite *Chigara*, an established high-level medium with whom he competes. *Chigara* refused to attend, saying that David had begun operating as a spirit-medium in his, *Chigara*'s territory, without asking permission. When the messenger brought the news to David/*Kafudzi* he was told that this was absolute nonsense owing to the fact that he, *Kafudzi*, was really more senior than *Chigara*.

Mobility

Korekore spirit-guardians are in a fixed relation one to another and their mediums cannot hope to increase the status of their spirit-guardians. In Chiota, however, mediums may be able to increase the status of their spirits by building up a sufficiently large sphere of influence.

Social Significance

Finally it is necessary to point out that Korekore mediums are dying out, while Zezuru ones are experiencing a rise in numbers and popularity. Garbett notes that many Korekore spirit-guardians are no longer represented by mediums and that the whole structure may well collapse with the death of the present Mutota medium.

It would appear, then, that the Korekore structure is not only more formalised than that of the Zezuru, but also more of a formality. That mediums are failing to come forward to replace others as they die suggests that mediumship among the Korekore no longer has the significance that it once had.

The Crux of the Difference

On the basis of the observed differences between the spirit-mediums of the Korekore and those of the Zezuru of Chiota, it would appear that while the Korekore situation represents a state of ossified charisma, the Zezuru mediums operate very much on the basis of personal charisma.

The temptation is to interpret one situation in terms of the other. That is to suggest either that the Chiota situation developed out of a disrupted Korekore-like situation or that the stable Korekore situation represents the routinisation of a Chiota-like situation, in much the way that Weber (1946 : 199) accounted for the development of the Christian church.

Today, the bishop, the priest, and the preacher are in fact no longer, as in early Christian times, holders of purely personal charisma. The supra-mundane and sacred values which they offer are given to everybody who seems worthy of them and who seeks for them. In former times, such leaders acted upon the personal command of their master; in principle they were responsible only to him. Nowadays, in spite of the partial survival of the old theory, such religious leaders are officials in the service of a functional purpose, which in the present-day 'church' has become routinised and, in turn, ideologically hallowed.

Zezuru flexibility and Korekore rigidity

The historical information that is available is inadequate to test conclusively either of these interpretations, and the reliable material which is available tends to refute the first. According to this interpretation, the Zezuru, prior to the arrival of the settlers had an hierarchical organisation of spirit-mediums. With the waxing of Christianity and the waning of 'traditional' religious practices following the rebellion of 1896 the structure was forgotten. When, in the early 1960s the traditional religion came to be revived, only very generalised ideas had survived, so that, lacking any structure, Zezuru mediums operated in something of a vacuum, competing with one another for popular support on the basis of personal charisma. Korekore, on the other hand, who did not experience the same religious upheavals, nor the rapid decline of 'traditional' practices, maintain the structure to the present day.

This interpretation would be feasible if it could be established that the Zezuru mediums were, in fact, hierarchically organised at the time the settlers arrived, in the early 1890s. The evidence points to the contrary, and comes from Ranger's (1967) analysis of the Shona and Matabele rebellion in 1896—7. The advantage of Ranger's work, from the point of view of this study, is that it describes and analyses a *social situation* with beliefs being used *in action* and is an excellent example of the way in which history can furnish the kinds of information commonly used in anthropological analysis.

According to Ranger's analysis, the Zezuru did not welcome the arrival of European settlers and missionaries in 1890, and in 1896, after a plague of locusts and an epidemic of rinderpest which wiped out most of their cattle, certain of their spirit-mediums interpreted this misfortune as being the result of European occupation. The only solution was to kill the settlers or drive them from the country. In this way, these spirit-mediums transformed the sentiment of protest from *vox populi* into *vox dei* as described above. They were charismatic figures whose relevant message was acceptable and accepted by the people.

Ranger argues that the mediums provided an organisational framework based on the existing '*Nehanda—Chaminuka*' hierarchy and the phenomenal rise to power of the medium of *Kagubi*, who had before the rebellion been a 'mere common or barn door Mondoro'. However Ranger is able to give no evidence for the existence of such an hierarchy and my own reading of the evidence suggests that the mediums who were involved in the rebellion formed an organisational framework based on the *ad hoc* patterns of relationships existing among them at that time. Indeed, the rise to fame of the *Kagubi* medium, and his ultimate ascendancy over the medium of the well-known spirit of *Nehanda* parallel so closely the story of David/*Kafudzi*, that it is a reasonable assumption to make that in 1896, just as in 1966, the rise of such figures was not so much the exception as the rule. As Ranger (1967 : 213) has said: 'One might speculate, indeed, that a constant theme of Shona political history has been the rise and fall of figures of this kind . . . '

The story of the Shona rebellion is one of order out of disorder, co-ordination

61

out of schism as the various autonomous petty chiefdoms of the Zezuru came to be united in collective action under the charismatic leadership of a number of their mediums. It is not the story of an established 'machine' of hierarchically arranged spirit-mediums.

While it is impossible to prove the hypothesis that the Korekore system is a development of a Chiota-like situation and quite probable that the present Chiota situation is not a degeneration of a Korekore-like rigidity, there remain two possible interpretations. First, that the differing religious systems of the two peoples is in some way associated with their different historical experiences and, second that they reflect contemporary difference of social structure. While the former speculation is essentially diachronic and the latter synchronic, it might be possible to argue that historical experience in so far as it is relevant to the present is also a synchronic variable.

History and religious structure

A significant difference between the Zezuru and the Korekore lies in their differ-ing historical experiences. While the former have never been united into any form of political confederacy, the Korekore are descended from the great Munhumu-tapa 'empire', which held sway in north-east Mashonaland during the sixteenth and seventeenth centuries. The existence of the Munhumutapa empire may have led to the development of an hierarchical religious order, which survived the dis-integration of that empire partly because its history still has significance for con-temporary Korekore society. Whereas Korekore history is rooted in ideas of hierarchy and imperial organisation, Zezuru history stresses the initiative of individuals as leaders. It is this emphasis on charismatic political authority which, I suggest, carries through into the religious life. It is also significant in the light of this suggestion, that the other great Shona empire centring around the Rozvi Changamire was also associated with a highly centralised religious cult, the Mwari or Mulimo cult, centred on certain caves out of which spoke the 'Voice of God'. This cult became the established religion of the Amandebele when they invaded Karangaland in the nineteenth century, and, Ranger argues, helped to foster Ndebele cohesion during the Matabele Rebellion of 1896.

The Munhumutapa dynasty was established in what is now north-east Mashonaland by invading Karanga people from the south in the fifteenth century. The leader of these Karanga invaders was Mutota, who had broken away from the existing Rozvi empire centred on Zimbabwe, near present day Fort Victoria. Mutota built up an extensive imperial organisation which is best described in the words of Gann (1965 : 9—10), who reports that the kingdom of Munhumutapa

became an empire over many other tribes who were allowed to keep their own chiefs but were obliged to forward tribute. In exchange the king's subjects re-ceived protection from their enemies, as well as gifts; the royal court perhaps acted as the centre of a vast system of tributary exchange which functioned with-

out money . . . The Monomotapas in time managed to build up a great tribal confederacy. Hoe-cultivation and small-scale industries like weaving, gold mining,
pottery and the production of ironware built up a surplus; trade in luxury goods
enhanced the country's wealth . . . The king himself used great nobles in his
household which formed the nucleus of a rudimentary state organisation. He also
received assistance from a body of tribal intellectuals, part royal spirit mediums
and part official historians, who were supposed to voice the will of ancestral
kings, and maintain the traditions of their race. There were too a host of office
bearers, described by the Portuguese chronicler of the sixteenth century as the
governor of the kingdoms, the captain-general, the chief major-domo, the chief
musician, the captain-general of the vanguard in wartime, the king's right hand,
the chief wizard, the king's doorkeeper, 'and numerous officers of lower rank
whom it would be unending and tedious to enumerate'. All these dignitaries held
land and vassals but they resided at the king's court . . . Local government remained in the hands of minor chiefs and headmen.

Abraham (1966 : 30) has shown from early Portuguese evidence that a spirit-
medium cult was flourishing in this empire. 'Antonio Bocarro states that the subjects of the Mutapa believe their kings go to heaven, and when they are there, call
them *muzimos* (*midzimu*) and ask them for whatever they require.' And most
writers on the role of the spirit-mediums amongst the Korekore at this time stress
its importance in maintaining the centrality of the empire.[3] Alpers (1968 : 13)
says:

The Mwene Mutapa was the ultimate religious authority in his kingdom for he
alone could communicate with the spirits of his ancestors . . . Indeed, the Mwene
Mutapa is sometimes described as being a divine king, in order to distinguish his
functions from that of a purely secular monarch . . . There was a close identification between the well-being of the Mwene Mutapa and the well-being of the
state. So long as he flourished, the kingdom would be blessed.

At the zenith of the Munhumutapa empire the nuclear area in present
Korekore land was firmly controlled by the Emperor and his close relatives, but
the outlying areas were governed by 'faithful followers' and it was one of these,
Changa who ruled from Zimbabwe, who built up a sufficiently large following in
that area to threaten the power of the Munhumutapa. During the seventeenth
century the power of the successors to Changa (the Changamires) increased,
while that of the Munhumutapa declined, in spite of, or because of, Portuguese
attempts to underpin the Munhumutapa empire.

Thus, by the late seventeenth century, the locus of power in what is now
Rhodesia shifted from the north-east to the south-west; that area which is now
Matabeleland, and Karangaland, and a new and prosperous state system devel-
oped, producing the marvellous stone architecture at Khami, Dhlo-Dhlo and
Nalatale which remains today.

Whereas the religious organisation of the Munhumutapa empire had centred
around their spirit-mediums, the Mwari cult of the Changamires 'was based upon
a different notion of how the living could establish contact with the divine'
(Ranger 1967 : 21), for in this system Mwari was contacted directly by the living

at certain shrines whence his voice emanated. Around the central shrine there was an elaborate organisation which included a series of messengers, (*wosana*), who served as intermediaries between the shrine and adherents of the cult in out-lying areas. Ranger (1967 : 23) has noted that this elaborate organisation 'ob-viously lent itself to the support of an experiment in political centralisation' and argues that the Rozvi Mambos fully appreciated the value of working with, or controlling this 'elaborate hierarchy', and that this is perhaps why they estab-lished their capital at Great Zimbabwe, which was also the central Mwari shrine.

Weinrich (1965 : 74) has also noted in her study of the Karanga of Chilimanzi that 'the most important source of power for the Rozvi king was his close associ-ation with the *Mwari* or High God cult through which he combined both politi-cal and religious power'.

Thus, there grew up, in both of these Shona states religious systems which were also centralised and hierarchical. The region lying between these two poles of political power was affected consecutively by them both and later by the in-vading Ndebele from the south. This region, which may be considered a no-man's-land between the two empires, is inhabited by the Zezuru, who themselves have no tradition of centralisation; quite the contrary in fact for Zezuru histories usually stress the individuality of historical figures who broke away from elder brothers and set up on their own. Relations between chiefdoms have never been hierarchical and centralised, but rather *ad hoc* dyadic relationships which have occasionally been cemented by marriage into a perpetual kinship link of *sekuru/ muzukuru* (mother's brother/sister's son) between the two lineages. Thus, the Nenguo lineage left the Chibi district in Karangaland under their leader Nooreka. Some of them remained in Mutoko, while others, under Kuwaradewe broke away again and settled in their present area. A woman of the Nenguo lineage was mar-ried by a member of the neighbouring Nyandoro people, so that all members of the Nenguo lineage refer to members of the Nyandoro lineage as 'sister's son', while the Nyandoro people reciprocate with 'mother's brothers'. Weinrich de-scribes a similar pattern among the Karanga, with the important difference that there, chiefs were obliged to seek permission to settle from the local ruling Rozvi chief, through whom they were incorporated into the centralised Rozvi adminis-tration.

Thus, in comparison with Karanga and Korekore history which stresses hier-archical patterns of political authority, Zezuru history stresses more the personal *charisma* of leaders who, on the basis of this personal power, were able to build up sufficiently large followings to be regarded as chiefs.

While a centralised hierarchical polity was associated, in the case of the Karanga and Korekore, to centralised and hierarchical religious organisations, the fluid political system of the Zezuru based on the autonomy of 'charismatic' chiefs and the development of *ad hoc* dyadic relationships between them, paral-led a correspondingly fluid religious organisation lacking in centrality. Indeed, it is difficult to conceive how the Zezuru, who jealously maintain the autonomy of their chiefs, could possibly subscribe to a centralised cult organisation such as that of the Korekore, which enshrines the opposite principles of super- and subordination, and the supremacy of one particular lineage, that of Mutota.

A tentative correlation has been established, then, between the political and religious orders amongst the Korekore and the Zezuru at least in terms of historical experience. But history is most relevant in sociological terms in the extent to which it is *perceived* by society, and to search for correlates of deeper sociological significance it is necessary to investigate contemporary aspects of social structures. After all, even given that political centralisation and religious centralisation may have been linked historically, it still remains to understand why it is that, in the case of the Korekore (and also the Karanga), centralised religious systems have survived the demise of corresponding political institutions. As Abraham (1966 : 45) has noted: 'After the death of Mutapa Nyamhandu, *c*. 1740, the Mutapa dynasty degenerated to provincial status in Thawara country west of Tete and became formally extinguished in 1902. The *mhondoro* cults associated with this dynasty did not fade away *pari passu* in the intervening period.'

Abraham (1966 : 46) himself attributed the survival of the spirit medium cult to its 'institutional vitality' and also to the importance of spirit-mediums as the carriers of historical knowledge. 'The Shona appear to have been permeated by a developed degree of historical consciousness – a consciousness that has outlived to some extent its political correlates. The *mhondoro* cults are major trace-elements precipitated by their history, and by their institutional arrangements to perpetuate awareness of the same.'

Garbett (1963a : 243) has related the survival of the spirit-medium organisation of the Korekore to the isolation of the habitat, which has helped to preserve beliefs intact, and also to the vagaries of climate and the rather poor physical environment. 'Korekore are faced continually by the threat of drought and famine.' However, it is an extremely dangerous procedure to try and explain religious structure in terms of ecological variables, and Garbett is forced to make the caveat 'given the Korekore belief in the powers of the spirit guardians'. This is a very big 'given' and, furthermore, it is difficult to explain the differences between Zezuru and Korekore in these terms. After all, Zezuru also complain about their environment, they also believe in the powers of their spirit-mediums, a belief which has survived their non-isolation, and yet their cult organisation is quite different.

The most important sociological variable which might be related to the difference in religious organisation is that of rate of change. Korekore were once great. Since the end of the sixteenth century, however, they have become increasingly marginal to major developments in Shona history with the locus of power shifting first to Karangaland and the Changamires and latterly to Zezuruland, Salisbury and the Europeans. Their remote geographical location in the Zambesi valley has effectively cut them off from the severest influence the colonial administration had in Chiota and other reserves proximate to Salisbury.

65

It is perhaps an overstatement to regard the Korekore as a stagnant society, living in the past, but it would nevertheless go some way to explaining the 'bureaucratisation' of the spirit-medium cult as part of the running down process. The mediums perpetuate the glorious past, which is changeless and as rigid as the cult organisation itself.

Another important factor is, no doubt, the lessening of the prestige of mediums which is implied in Garbett's report that new mediums are no longer coming forward to fill vacancies left by dying mediums. Spirit-mediums seem to be losing their social significance in Korekoreland, and indeed, one of their main functions, the selection of new chiefs, has been whittled away by the colonial administration.

In contrast to the Korekore, the Zezuru are very much in the front line of 'progress' in Rhodesia. Their history does not stress one charismatic figure and subsequent routinisation — it stresses individual initiative and the constant bursting up of charismatic energy. This is the state of Chiota now. For them no lifeless religious organisation, but a cult of great vigour and carrying great prestige, mainly because of the rise of cultural nationalism in the area (see chapter 6). Not only is there severe competition to replace dead mediums, but there are always plenty of aspirant mediums claiming to be possessed by new spirits. The contrast, then, is between on the one hand a stagnant conservative society and, on the other, the dynamic and radical Zezuru.

Demographic factors play a part in reinforcing this difference because the relatively low population density of the Korekore, coupled with poorly developed communications in the area, militate against the possibility of spirit-mediums being able to build up 'spheres of influence', based upon personal authority as do the mediums of Chiota where the population is ten times as dense and communications comparatively good.

The nature of the differences between Zezuru and Korekore society and spirit-medium organisation recalls Douglas' (1970) analysis of trance among the Nuer and Dinka in *Natural Symbols*. She relates the different attitudes to trance in the two societies to the varying incidence of two social structural variables, grid and group. While the Nuer regard trance as dangerous and the Dinka regard it as benign, the former society presents a greater emphasis on group boundaries and on social categories than the latter. The material that has been presented for the Shona case suggests that the Korekore are much more concerned with *controlling* spirit-mediumship than are the Zezuru. At the same time, it has been noted that there has been a greater incidence of social and economic change amongst the Zezuru and that social experience is not rigidly controlled in terms of groups (i.e. lineages) or categories, (i.e. age, sex) as it was, or as that of the Korekore is.

Very tentatively, then, it is suggested that the difference in religious organisation of the two peoples is related to the degree of control exercised in each, and that the religious life is controlled in proportion to the amount of control over social experience in its wider aspect. While the Zezuru experience rapid change, and unpredictable future, rapid economic or political success on the basis of personal charisma, and diminishing control in terms of grid and group, so their religious life features dynamic charismatic spirit-mediums and a highly fluid and little-controlled pantheon of spirits. The Korekore, on the other hand, represent a much more static state of affairs, where the old groups and categories continue to control social experience. This fact is reflected in the emphasis they place on their centralised past, and on their religious belief in a hierarchy of spirits coupled to a constant striving to control spirit-mediumship.

5

Spirit-mediums in ritual action

One of the most significant contributions of the Manchester School to social anthropology was the new and greater emphasis that they gave to detailed case material. Gluckman (1958), Mitchell (1956), Victor Turner (1957) with his development of the notion of social drama and others did not present their readers with ready-made models illustrated by what van Velsen (1967) called 'apt illustrations'; their analyses of the regularities of social life were derived from the observation and reporting of situations in which people were actually handling their structural relationships.

While it is probably true that the majority of anthropologists in fact develop their analysis from this kind of information, apart from that obtained by formal interviews, village censuses etc . . . , the members of the Manchester School gave the reader this basic information so that he could not only see for himself how social organisation actually worked, but also challenge the author's analysis should he so wish. The presentation of this type of (almost) raw field material was also a move towards greater intellectual honesty.

Up until now this book has proceeded on what might be called pre-Manchester lines. The reader has been given a 'competence' in Zezuru custom and an analytical model which tries to make overall sense of religious belief and the sociology of spirit-mediumship. However, the material on which this analysis is based was basically a series of social situations and extended case histories, for not only was it extremely difficult to gather other types of information (see above p. 2), but the aims of my investigation were to ascertain not so much the ideals of the people of Chiota in relation to their religious beliefs and practices as the way in which these ideals were put to use. I could not begin my analysis with this kind of raw material simply because it only makes sense once the meanings of certain concepts and symbols have been grasped.

In this chapter I set out to describe and analyse the events which occurred in and around the village of Tatenda over a two-year period. This particular case was chosen because it involves a number of dramatic situations in which spirit-mediums played an important role. The entry into high-level spirit-mediumship of my assistant, Thomas Mutero, was long drawn-out and difficult, for not only did he meet considerable opposition in the village from the senior low-level village medium, Andrew, but he also became involved in a long-standing dispute between his full brother, John and his paternal half-brother, James. The case traces events in the village following the death of Rufu who was the father of

James, John and Thomas, and leads to the hiving off of John and Thomas who is installed in his own ritual house as a high-level spirit-medium. Because Thomas came into contact with two other established high-level mediums, this case also contains material relating to religious organisation over and above village level.

The extended case method and situational analysis have a number of serious drawbacks which relate to the difficulties involved in obtaining all information which might be relevant. In the first place, the observer cannot be omnipresent; he witnesses only a part of the complex reality around him. More serious, perhaps, than geographical position, is his social position which restricts his access to information. This was especially so in the case which follows for because Thomas was my field assistant I was denied a similar close contact with his political and religious rivals, James and Andrew. Secondly, the observer's perception of the material with which he is confronted is severely constrained by his intellectual training and his personal interest, and finally, when he comes to write down that which he has observed, he is obliged to prune and pare for stylistic reasons. In short, participant observation has its drawbacks as well as its advantages. The observer must be constantly aware of the distortions that might occur in his material. In the narrative that follows, I have tried always to make my own situation clear for this reason.

The narrative has been set down in chronological order and it is broken from time to time for analytical comment. At the end I have singled out what I consider its most interesting aspects for further comment. I have chosen to use the proper names of persons and to state the genealogical relationships where relevant, but this information, and that relating to spirit-mediums and their possessing spirits is available in the two genealogies on pages 72–3 and 74–5. The letter and number codes following names refer to the position of that person in Genealogy 1.

The history of the village: *dramatis personae*

Mutero (C3) (*mutupo*: Shave: *chidawo*: Museyamwa) was a member of the Mutekedza royal lineage who lived in a distrist of Rhodesia known as Njanja in the valley of the Sabi river. He gave up his and his descendant's rights in the Mutekedza chieftainship by taking up residence in the chieftaincy of Nenguo.[1] He was a *nganga* and had been responsible for removing a very serious *ngozi* affliction from the Nenguo lineage. In gratitude and payment, the then chief Nenguo gave him two of his 'sisters' as wives (C2, C4) and rights to farm an area of land in his chieftaincy. He became the chief's son-in-law, and his present agnatic descendants thus refer to all members of the Nenguo lineage as 'mother's brothers' (*vasekuru*).[2]

On his death, his senior son (*nevanje*) Tatenda (D2) succeeded to his position as 'father' (*baba*) of the lineage. He was recognised as an official village headman

69

(*sabuku*), thus giving the village its present name. He was pre-deceased by his full brother Mamire (D5), who was killed by lightning. His wife (D4) declined to be inherited (*gara nhaka*) by either her husband's full-brother, Tatenda, or his half-brother, Rufu (D7), and left for her natal village in the chieftaincy of chief Chiota, taking her children with her. They still live there, and we shall be concerned in particular with her two sons, Naison (E16) and Matthew (E17) later in the narrative.

On the death of Tatenda, the title of father of the family and headship of the village passed to his half-brother, Rufu. He himself became a man of great wealth and prominence in the community, but after the compulsory de-stocking of cattle in 1947, he transferred the cash that accrued to his eldest son, James (E22). Although he remained the father of the family, he passed on the office of village headman to Andrew (E14), one of the sons of Tatenda. But Andrew was only the *de jure* head of the village, for although he was responsible for judging cases in the village, collecting taxes and acting as the chief's representative, no decisions could be reached without consultation with Rufu.

The village then consisted of the sons of Tatenda and Rufu and their wives, with the exception of Simon (E3) who lived on his farm in the Native Purchase Area (NPA) of Muda in Mount Darwin. In addition were various daughters who were either widowed or divorced or as yet unmarried, and the descendants of Mutero's daughter, Namiso (D10), who were the senior *vazukuru* (sister's sons) in the village. Men who had houses in the village were not always present. James spent most of his time at his shop in Wedza, while John (E43) was mostly in Salisbury where he worked as a medical orderly for one of the big tobacco companies. Christopher (E32) was a builder on the nearby European farms, so was often away also. Moses (E9), Manyuchi (E5) and Andrew had given up work in town and were permanent residents, as were Phineas (E52), and Sebastian (D11), the son and husband of Namiso.

Apart from Naison and Matthew mentioned earlier, other non-residents of Tatenda retained close ties and played important roles in the conduct of affairs, in particular the female members of the family who lived away with their husbands. Notable amongst these were James' sister Ruth (E24) who practised as a *nganga* some six miles from the village, Andrew's sister, Tenzeni (E11), who lived with her husband Matabini (E12), a member of the Nyandoro royal lineage, in the Nyandoro chieftaincy, John's sisters Carmen (E39), married and living in Salisbury, and Helen (E41), married and living some two miles away from Tatenda. The descendants of Rufu's sisters, Rowesa (D13) and Amashava (D12), living at Wedza and in the Mudzimerema chieftaincy respectively were important from time to time. They, like the descendants of Namiso were important as *vazukuru*.

In addition John's matrilateral relatives played leading roles. They are Veronica (E55), John's mother's younger sister (*amai nini*), married to Choto

(E54) the eldest son of Amashava, and John's mother's mother's younger sister and her classificatory son, Joni Chiota, living in the chiefdom of chief Chiota.

The religious situation in the village was quite simple. Three descendants of Mutero were spirit-mediums. Margaret (E1), a daughter of Tatenda, was host to Mutero's younger brother, *Zvichauya* (C5), Ruth was host to Mutero's father, *Maingano* (B1) while Andrew acted as host to *Maingano*'s younger brother, *Mavu*. Andrew, although not possessed by the most senior ancestor, spirit was regarded as the senior medium in the village and he was consulted by the villagers about their problems. Although Andrew was officially village headman, most of his prestige in the village derived from his status as senior spirit-medium.

Tatenda represents, then, a simple commoner village, with a patrilineal core founded by Mutero and small families linked to this by matrilateral ties. The descendants of Mutero are themselves subdivided into segments. There are the three main houses (*dzimba*) founded by Mutero's three sons and these are in turn segmented according to these sons' respective wives. As was pointed out in chapter 1 the solidarity of such lineages without an interest in an important office is very weak and is prejudiced by the greater solidarity of their component segments. Already, when I arrived to stay in the village as guest of Thomas (E47), there had developed a considerable antagonism between James and his full siblings and John and his.

My presence at this time in Tatenda village affected the situation I was studying in a number of ways and because Thomas was my paid assistant and interpreter (through his tutelage I became sufficiently proficient in the language not to need him as interpreter after a time) and was the guest of his brother John, I came by their side of the story much more easily than that of James. At this time my presence in Chiota was still regarded by most people with the greatest suspicion and the people of Tatenda suffered considerable hardship as a result. Once the village was threatened with arson on my account, but Andrew claimed that the village had been saved from certain destruction by the spirit *Mavu* of which he was medium. *Mavu*, he said, had awakened him in the night just in time to frighten off a gang of youths who had arrived to set fire to the houses.

Whilst the whole village had to suffer for my presence, Thomas took the lion's share of the difficulties. His role as intermediary between myself and the people required a lot of courage and good faith. In exchange for a monthly salary, he valiantly introduced me to the people I wanted to meet and defended my interests as best he could. I was given a bed in John's house and ate food prepared by his divorced sister, Anna (E37). In exchange for this, I provided the household with supplies of tea, milk, sugar and bread. I felt that Thomas's subsequent entry into spirit-mediumship was not unlinked with the fact that he was my assistant, but more of that later.

The account of the events which led up to the situation which I was to witness came from John and Thomas.

71

A

B

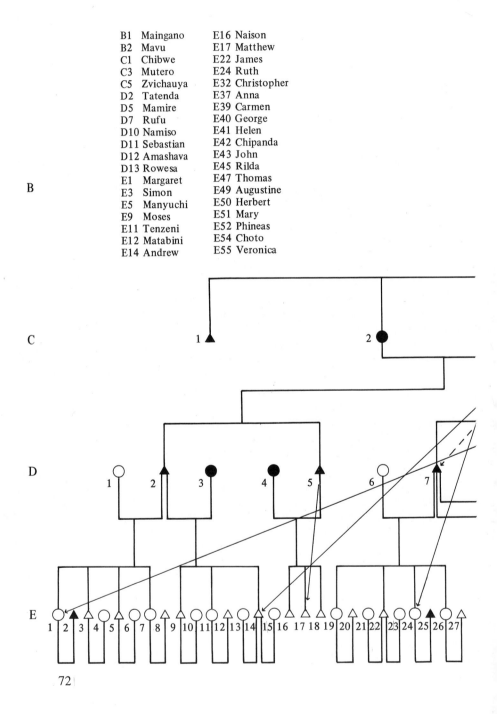

B1 Maingano
B2 Mavu
C1 Chibwe
C3 Mutero
C5 Zvichauya
D2 Tatenda
D5 Mamire
D7 Rufu
D10 Namiso
D11 Sebastian
D12 Amashava
D13 Rowesa
E1 Margaret
E3 Simon
E5 Manyuchi
E9 Moses
E11 Tenzeni
E12 Matabini
E14 Andrew

E16 Naison
E17 Matthew
E22 James
E24 Ruth
E32 Christopher
E37 Anna
E39 Carmen
E40 George
E41 Helen
E42 Chipanda
E43 John
E45 Rilda
E47 Thomas
E49 Augustine
E50 Herbert
E51 Mary
E52 Phineas
E54 Choto
E55 Veronica

C

D

E

72

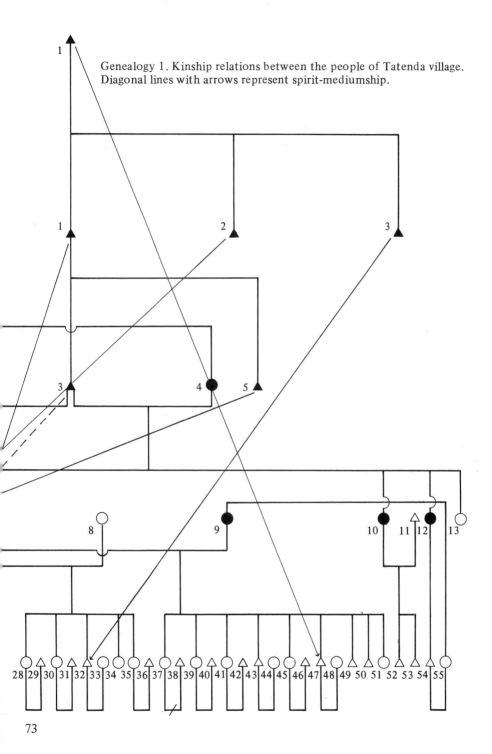

Genealogy 1. Kinship relations between the people of Tatenda village. Diagonal lines with arrows represent spirit-mediumship.

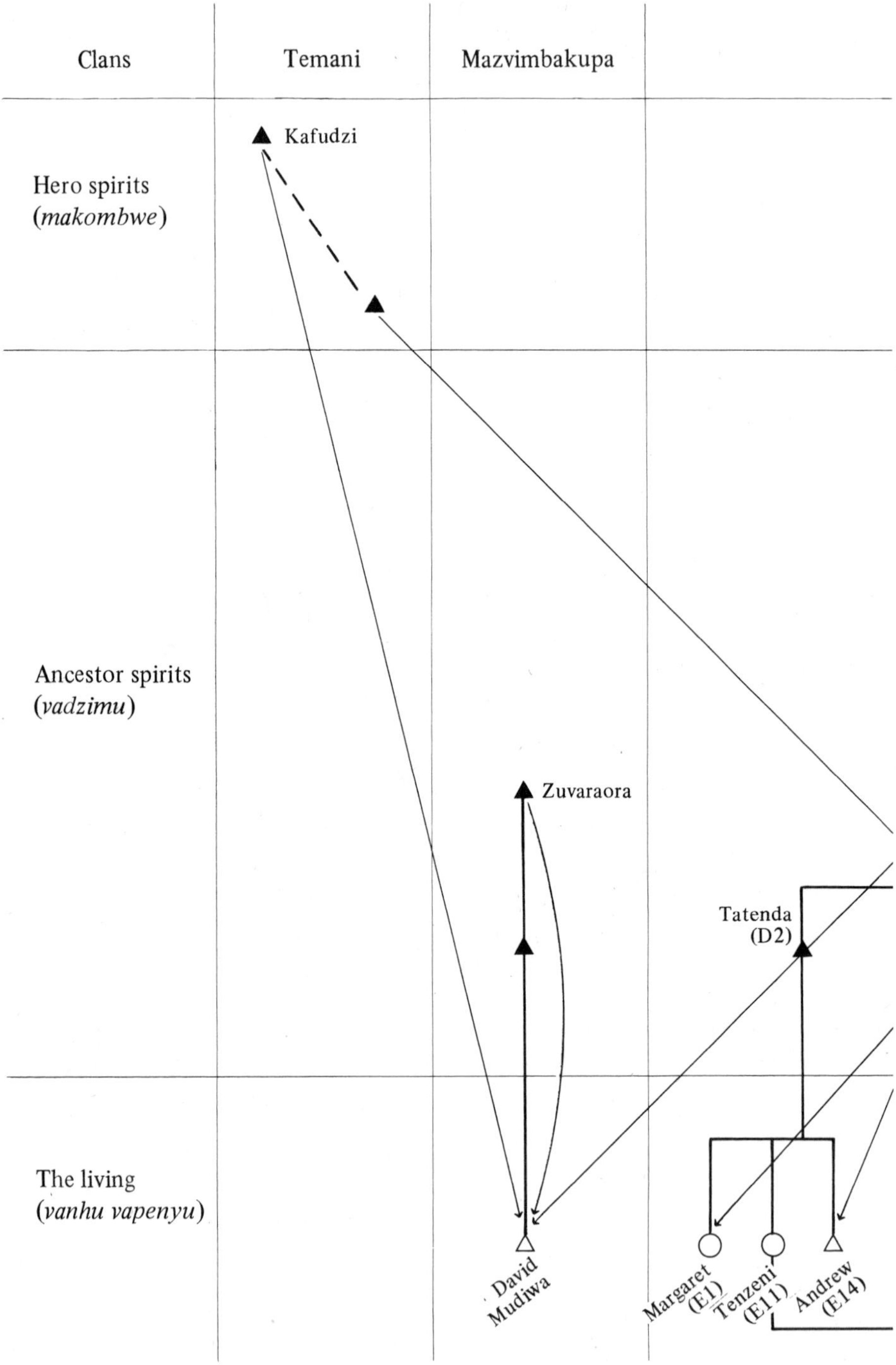

Clans	Temani	Mazvimbakupa	

Hero spirits
(*makombwe*)

▲ Kafudzi

▲

Ancestor spirits
(*vadzimu*)

▲ Zuvaraora

Tatenda
(D2)
▲

The living
(*vanhu vapenyu*)

△ David
Mudiwa

○ Margaret
(E1)

○ Tenzeni
(E11)

△ Andrew
(E14)

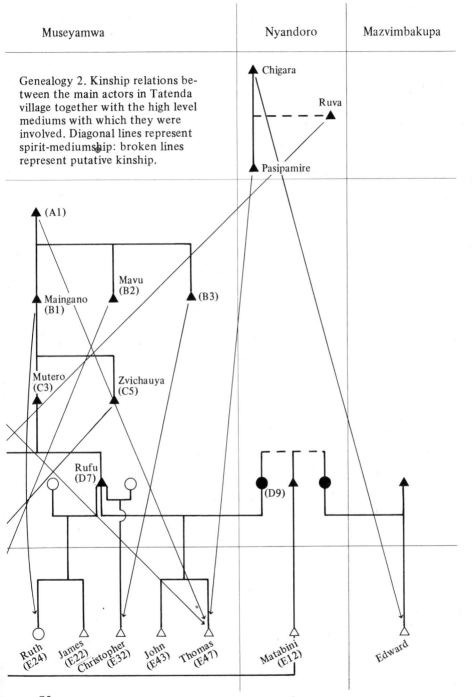

Museyamwa | Nyandoro | Mazvimbakupa

Genealogy 2. Kinship relations between the main actors in Tatenda village together with the high level mediums with which they were involved. Diagonal lines represent spirit-mediumship: broken lines represent putative kinship.

Chigara

Ruva

Pasipamire

(A1)

Mavu (B2)

(B3)

Maingano (B1)

Mutero (C3)

Zvichauya (C5)

Rufu (D7)

(D9)

Ruth (E24)

James (E22)

Christopher (E32)

John (E43)

Thomas (E47)

Matabini (E12)

Edward

The genesis of the dispute

John's mother (D9) died soon after the birth of her ninth child, and so her eldest daughter, Anna, took on the responsibility of caring for the rest of the children. When Anna was married and went to live with her husband in the Mudzimerema chiefdom, Carmen took over these duties although Anna had numbers of her siblings to stay. This generosity did not please Anna's husband, and it was one of the reasons why he divorced her after she had borne him one son. Most of the bridewealth he had paid was returned to him by Rufu, which according to John amounted to seven cattle and £10. Anna returned to Tatenda village where she has remained ever since as 'mother' to her siblings.

John claimed that their mother's death brought them a great deal of hardship, and that their father took more interest in his children by other wives. This assessment was corroborated by other people who had known John at this time and who agreed that their poverty had been remarkable even by Chiota standards.

John decided that as he was the eldest son it was up to him to provide for his siblings, so he took himself to school at the Methodist mission of Waddilove, where he earned his school fees by working for the staff during term-time and the holidays. However, during the time that he was studying for standard VI he became ill from time to time, feeling faint and having to leave his lessons, and went to consult his sister, Ruth, who was able to cure him. However, John felt that he could no longer continue in school so went to stay in Wedza with James (who owned a shop, purchased and stocked with the money he had been given by Rufu). There he had a very hard time and found himself frequently left in charge of the shop for long periods while James took time off. He earned little more than his keep, which he thought out of proportion to the amount of work he was doing, so he told James that he wanted to go home to discuss his future with their father, Rufu. James tried to persuade him to stay, telling him that the shop belonged to all of them, as the capital had all been provided by their father when his cattle had been compulsorily purchased. If John stayed with him then he would become a full partner and have his own business one day. John was adamant, and decided to leave, but had to walk the thirty miles home when James refused to give him money for his bus fare.

On arriving home John told his father he would like to join the police force. Although Rufu was not in favour he went to Salisbury and joined up. However, he quickly found he could not work, due to mysterious symptoms which cleared up as soon as he left. He found that every time he looked for work the symptoms recurred. He returned home on a bicycle, lent to him by Garmen's husband George (E40), and saw his father who told him that his illness was due to his having gone against his (father's) word. He returned to town and stopped on the road overcome with fatigue and worry. Along the road came James in his lorry and about six people. He did not stop for his brother, but merely waved. John broke down and wept, finally managing to reach town on foot. From then onwards John's health and finances improved. After a number of vicissitudes he found work as a telephone operator in a firm in Salisbury and soon was promoted in recognition of his ability not only in operating the telephone exchange but also in getting on with his European employers.

He was now able to send his younger siblings, Thomas and Mary (E51), to school (indeed this was one of the reasons he had decided to curtail his own education at standard VI). Herbert (E50), his younger brother, went to live with Carmen in Salisbury. After a year or two as a telephone operator, John applied to train as an orderly at Harare hospital. He was accepted, and two years later he passed out and began working in a government clinic. He then acquired a job in a tobacco firm, where he earned £27 per month, which was, by Rhodesian African standards, a good salary.

In 1963 John married. He went to his father for the necessary cash, it being generally agreed that a father should provide the bridewealth for each of his sons' first wives. However, the money was not forthcoming. John claimed that when his sister Carmen was married, Rufu had set aside the incoming bridewealth for his, John's, marriage. The money was given to James for safe-keeping. When John went to James to demand this, he was told that he had received it all in assistance for his education. This John denied, saying that out of a total of £35, he had only received £10. There was still £25 outstanding. Ultimately John was obliged to provide the money himself.

John's major grievances, then, were based on what he considered to be selfish behaviour on James' part. In the matter of the cash from the destocked cattle and from Carmen's marriage James had diverted what was really common property to his own private use.

It is interesting to note that John himself saw all his misfortunes as deriving from his mother's premature death. He claimed that as a general rule in polygynous households mothers support their children before their husbands and ensure that they are properly cared for. In this case James had benefited not only because he was the eldest son, but also because his mother had supported him. The husband of John's full sister, Helen, who could usually be counted on to express the same opinion as John in such matters, claimed that James' mother had brought about John's mother's death through the use of witchcraft.

But John had begun to redress the balance, and through hard work he had himself become something of a rich man. He now owned a car worth some £100 and his income was sufficient for him to buy good clothes and to eat well. Furthermore, due to his policy of educating his younger brothers, these were now partially self-sufficient and their success added further to the lustre of their 'house'. Thomas had passed his form II and was now a school teacher, Augustine (E49) had won a scholarship to Goromonzi Secondary School and only Herbert was still dependent and living with Carmen.

Whilst John's fortunes had waxed, those of James had waned. By June of 1964 his fleet of six lorries had been reduced to one battered Chevrolet truck, one of his stores had closed down and the grinding mill which he had bought in the Nyandoro chiefdom was broken and out of order. John and Thomas did not try to conceal their pleasure at the swing of fortune in their favour.

As later events were to show, the tenuous cohesion in the village was being maintained by the continued presence of Rufu, whose age and wisdom commanded respect from all.

Rufu's death

On 16 June 1964 after a sudden deterioration in health, the old man died, having first dictated his outstanding debts and credits to Thomas, in the company of James, John, Andrew, Manyuchi, Moses and Christopher.

The funeral (*guva*) was lavish and lasted several days during which relatives both close and distant came to the village to pay their respects and to partake of the large amount of food and beer provided.[3] The costs were met by James, John and Christopher and the three cattle which were killed for meat were provided by Christopher, by Rufu's senior son-in-law and his sister's son, Phineas.

The first funeral rite ended, as is customary, with the distribution of the dead man's personal effects (*kuparadza nhumbi*) and the appointment of a regent to act as father of the family until the second funerary rite of *kurova guva* to be held about a year later. On this occasion, Rufu's brother's son, Naison, was appointed regent largely because he lived outside Tatenda village and had no claims himself to the office.

This was undoubtedly a turning point in the fortunes of Tatenda village; it is generally acknowledged that the death of old men brings in its train subsequent quarrellings between the children and the collapse of any sort of unity that might have been maintained during their lifetime. The remarks of a local store-keeper whose village was adjacent to Tatenda are germane:

Just look at that village. There is really going to be quarrelling there. If you can be around for *kurova guva*,I suggest you attend, because then all the quarrels will come out into the open. John, Christopher and James are all interested in Rufu's inheritance. James was given a lot of money by Rufu when his cattle were sold during the destocking [late 1940s] and the other sons are envious and want their share. Just look at that scotch-cart. It is just sitting there and rotting. No one wants to repair it for then all the others will use it. It is their common property until *kurova guva* when it will finally be decided who should inherit it. Yes, there is trouble in that village. The house (*imba*) of James is coming down in the world while the other two (those of John and Christopher) are coming up.

The problems of inheritance and succession, raised by the death of Rufu, led to a build up in the tension between John and James, for John realised at *kurova guva* he had the chance to claim back the bridewealth, which he believed James to have misappropriated. He also resented the near certainty that at this rite

James would be appointed to the position of his dead father, thus assuming authority over his siblings, John included.

Thus the death of Rufu reduced the village to a state of suspended animation until *kurova guva* and the final dispersal of Rufu's property and offices. Also, Rufu's death put a ritual prohibition on the village. No ritual could be held until *kurova guva*.[4]

The rite of *kurova guva* has a dual function, for not only is it the occasion for the distribution of property and offices of the dead man. It is also the time when the dead man's spirit is brought back into the company of the lineage, as a fully fledged ancestor spirit (*mudzimu*). Up to this time, it is believed to have no say in lineage affairs and roams around alone. It may not punish on its own behalf but if *kurova guva* is delayed too long, the other lineage ancestors may permit affliction to strike as warning that the rite is overdue. The normal period between death and *kurova guva* is one year. The final ritual of *kudzurura guva* is held some time after *kurova guva*, and is the ritual of final incorporation of the new spirit into the ranks of the lineage dead.

The onset and initial social consequences of Thomas's afflictions

Soon after the death of Rufu, Thomas began to exhibit disquieting symptoms. He was overcome with fits of depression during which it was difficult to communicate with him, and by the end of June 1964 he had become allergic to home-brewed beer, the sight or smell of which made him vomit. The allergy soon extended to cover petrol fumes also, so that he could not travel by car without vomiting. Prior to this Thomas enjoyed beer drinks and had frequently travelled in cars.

On 6 July Thomas, on his own initiative, decided to consult a spirit-medium as to the cause of these symptoms. His classificatory mother's brother, Joni Chiota led us to a little known female medium living near his own village. After being given 3 shillings, she took snuff and fell into a trance with a slight shudder. After the medium in trance had been greeted, Thomas asked why it was that he was troubled by cars and beer. The medium first asked questions concerning the death of Rufu, implying that this might have some bearing. Thomas immediately scotched this idea by stating that he had had trouble before the death of his father. He was also asked about his relations with girls and then told the best thing to do was to buy finger millet (*zvio*), a cloth (*jira*) and a knife (*banga*), for the spirit which was troubling him and to hold a formal ritual (*bira*) for the ancestors at Tatenda village. I was unable to learn much more from Thomas about the seance: he said he had been told the same thing by an *nganga* previously, and that he had had similar allergies before the death of his father.

However, nothing was done about it and by the end of August the allergy had extended even further, to include the written word, onions, white bread, butter, margarine, tea, and stiff porridge (*sadza*) made out of maize. The consequences were considerable. First it meant that he had to have a special diet of coffee and brown bread in the morning and either *sadza* made of millet or rice as his staple. This latter involved his sister Anna in considerably more work because finger millet cannot be satisfactorily ground at the grinding mill; it has to be ground by hand after being roasted. Within his own homestead, then, Thomas was one set apart by his dietary regulations, a fact that no-one could fail to notice.

These allergies and the others also affected his relations with the public at large. No longer could he sit with people at beer drinks. He had to sit apart lest he should smell the beer or tobacco smoke. If anyone happened to light a cigarette in his presence he would ostentatiously withdraw. In most cases the guilty party apologised and extinguished his tobacco, for it is generally accepted that this particular allergy is a symptom of spirit possession.

My own relationship with Thomas was also affected. Beer drinks were the main social activities in those long dry winter months and because Thomas was obliged to sit well beyond the odours of the beer, I found myself alone and unable to converse properly. His sickness on trying to read meant that he was no longer able to keep a diary or to help me with genealogy collecting. In effect his difficulties made our relationahip unviable and, significantly, publicly so. Thomas was my assistant yet, at the same time, was not. I felt at the time that his condition was a neurotic response to the impossible social situation in which he found himself. But the implications went well beyond his relationship with me.

Thomas's difficulties increased. By November the allergy had extended to meat so that he was reduced to a vegetarian diet. He became more and more drawn into himself as social relations became the more difficult to sustain. He spent a long period alone in the bush and began to learn to play the thumb-piano (*mbira*). Bit by bit the dietary restrictions had forced him to abandon many of his customary activities.

The responsibility for effecting a 'cure' fell to John, as Thomas's eldest brother, although Naison as the stand-in for their dead father, Rufu, was kept informed of developments. John was determined that Thomas should be restored to some sort of normality as soon as possible, not least in order that he might be able to fulfil his obligations as my assistant, or at least to be able to teach again. As yet there was no mention of the possibility that Thomas might become a 'high-level' medium. For my part I was equally determined that things should be put right rapidly or else I should have to find a new assistant. My mentioning this to John and Thomas met with no enthusiasm, and they determined to do all in their power to bring about a reduction in the allergies.

Consultations took place between John and Thomas and Andrew/*Mavu*, for the whole village recognised Andrew as being the senior medium and *Mavu* the *mudzimu*, to be consulted on all matters of importance. Andrew/*Mavu* said that first they should perform the rite of *kudzurura guva* for Rufu's two dead sisters, Namiso and Mandireva. This was duly executed in October 1964. He further suggested that Thomas was about to become a medium and that he was being troubled by an unknown spirit. Although no ritual could be held to induce possession until after *kurova guva* for Rufu, he thought that if certain things were bought and dedicated to the spirit, there would be some abatement of the allergies. John therefore bought a black dog, a black bed sheet for Thomas and a ritual knife. At a brief ceremony in the house of Christopher's mother, in which Rufu had died, Andrew knelt in front of the cooking pots and, clapping his hands, asked whoever it might be who was causing the trouble to desist.[5] The allergies continued without abatement.

The situation persisted like this until I left Tatenda village in November 1964. I had decided that I must live elsewhere since relations with Thomas were impossible. I also hoped that much of the veiled hostility which I had encountered in the vicinity of Tatenda village might be peculiar to the area and that I should do better elsewhere with an assistant from outside Chiota reserve. Having severed formal links with Tatenda, relations with Thomas improved and I managed to keep in touch with subsequent developments although then living some ten miles away.

In November 1964, Thomas's troubles increased. Having made a schoolgirl pregnant, he was forced into marrying her by his elder brothers. He himself was opposed to the marriage, but gave way to his elder brothers who pointed out that if he did not marry her the damages would be considerable and that the family name would be disgraced. Teachers who despoil schoolgirls find it difficult to obtain teaching posts again anyway.

In January 1965, Thomas regained his post at Mahusekwa School having succeeded in overcoming his allergy to the written word. I do not know how this was effected. Up to this stage, Thomas's affliction had been primarily the concern of his full brother John, but the other brothers had been involved and had certainly seen no reason to be sceptical. Andrew/*Mavu* had been consulted at every turn, although little progress towards a resolution of the condition had been made. Subsequent events were to change all this.

John's illness

On Sunday 4 April John was taken by car from his town house in Salisbury to the village of David Mudiwa, a high-level medium (see Genealogy 2). The previous day, after a bout of 'flu, John had woken to find that his legs were totally paralysed, and that he was in a generally weak condition. From the first, so he told me, he had no intention of going to the hospital, and although he was a medical orderly and had a good knowledge of Western medicine, he was quite convinced that this disaster was an 'African illness' (*chirwere che chivanhu*, literally, an illness of the people). He had been taken by his wife to consult a female spirit-medium living in the same street and she had advised him to consult David

81

Mudiwa. He telephoned Mahusekwa and his brother-in-law, Chipanda, and Thomas went to town to bring him to the medium's village.

David Mudiwa, who was introduced in chapter 3, was at this time only beginning his career as a spirit-medium. He was still operating in his first small seance house (*banya*) and his reputation was still restricted to the people living in and near his own village and a few satisfied clients who had visited him from Salisbury. The woman who had sent John from Salisbury had been initiated by him.

John's case was certainly the most difficult he had yet encountered, but he took him in and soon began enquiries as to the causes of the sickness. He first of all made mention of the fact that there was an outstanding ritual to be performed in Tatenda. This was confirmed by Thomas who said that *kurova guva* for their father, Rufu, had not yet been performed. The following day further enquiries were made in the presence of John's wife, four of his full-sisters, Carmen, Filda (E45), Anna and Helen and her husband, Chipanda (E42). Thomas was also present as was the younger sister of his mother, Veronica, and a classificatory mother's brother, Majoni.

The divination centred around the activities of John's wife, who was asked if she used love medicine (*mufuwhira*). At first she denied it (as do nearly all women who are similarly accused) but finally she was forced to confess by the obvious anger of David/*Kafudzi* and the prodding of Carmen, who seemed delighted to see her in such embarrassing circumstances. When asked how she came by it, she replied that her mother gave it to her before she died. David/*Kafudzi* was not satisfied and pressed the point, telling her that she had surely also obtained it from other people. Who were they? By this time she was showing signs of extreme stress and began to weep. David/*Kafudzi* and Carmen both urged her to confess, while others sat around passively, notably John who seemed quite withdrawn. Ultimately she capitulated and confessed that she had been given it by her mother's younger sister. Still David/*Kafudzi* was not satisfied and with further pressing she admitted that she had been given it by her elder sister. But then, doubtless appreciating that the implications of all this questioning were that she had poisoned her husband, she said that she had not used it after her marriage. David/*Kafudzi* expressed his disbelief as did Carmen, who, gloating over the plight of her sister-in-law, continued to urge her to confess. The poor wife now broke down almost completely under the strain, hardly able to control herself for her tears and hopeless anger. John and the *mbira* player very gently told her that they were not bringing a case against her (*hasina moswa* literally, there is no case) and that she would do better to answer all questions honestly. It was best, they said, to clear up all these little things. David/*Kafudzi* then turned to her and asked her if she had other men apart from John. She denied this and then, in a flurry of sobs, convulsions and tears, she blurted out that she did not want to eat her husband. '*Handisikuda kudya murume wangu. Handisi muroyi. Ini, handisi muHera.*' (I do not want to eat my husband. I am not a witch. I am not a Hera woman — this was a retaliation against Carmen who is a Hera woman).

82

'If you think I am a witch', she continued, 'then I will wipe out your whole lineage (*dzinza*).' At this stage, David/*Kafudzi* left them alone, while John's wife muttered to herself 'You are maltreating me; I am no young girl . . .'

It rather looked as if the divination was closing in on John's wife, but afterwards, Carmen told me in a hushed voice that it was really James who was at the bottom of everything and also the ancestors (*vadzimu varipasi*, literally, the ancestors are on the ground). She enjoined me not to divulge this confidence to anyone.

This divination is interesting from a number of points of view, not least the way in which David/*Kafudzi* by the use of subtle questions managed to close in on the sorts of factors which his clients were themselves considering as possible causes. Subsequent divinations began to place the blame on James himself, but we shall return to this later. At this stage, Carmen, Filda and Anna were quite happy to believe that John's wife had given him poison. There is general tension in the brother's sister/brother's wife relationship amongst the Zezuru and this is a clear example of its being given content. However, John was not himself happy with this divination. He loved his wife and was not prepared to believe her anything but faithful to him. He preferred the later diagnosis that James was somehow responsible. Indeed, even if Carmen herself believed John's wife to have been guilty this did not preclude her believing in James' guilt also. In spite of these different views as to the cause of the trouble, all were united in believing that it would be advisable to perform *kurova guva* as soon as possible.

Significantly, no-one, apart from his close family, had visited John at the medium's home. The absence of Andrew and James and the others from Tatenda has been noticed as being conspicuous. This only served to confirm Thomas and John in their view that James was somehow responsible. Why else would he not come to visit his brother? The only other agnate who did pay a visit was Christopher who was to remain impartial throughout.

A seance in Ruth's house

But the rest of the village was not remaining wholly passive and on the night of 6 April a seance was organised at the house of James' full sister, Ruth. I was not present at this seance, but Chipanda informed me that most of Tatenda village, with the exception of John, Thomas and their close kin had been present. Andrew, Ruth, Margaret and Moses' wife went into trance as did Christopher for the first time. The most notable event of the seance was Andrew/*Mavu*'s reaction to recent events. After complaining that John should never have been taken to consult a strange spirit-medium before asking his, *Mavu*'s permission, and having also said that Christopher should not have fallen into trance on that occasion, he took three large calabashes which were being used as sounding boards for the thumb-piano and smashed them on the floor. Chipanda thought that this sign of anger on the part of the ancestors was due not to John's behaviour, but to that of James. John felt no guilt and claimed that he could not possibly continue to consult Andrew/*Mavu* for the simple reason that he was unwilling to expose the deep causes of the affliction. Andrew/*Mavu* would be ashamed (*kunyara*) to tell the 'truth'.

Andrew/*Mavu*'s action at this seance is also interesting from the medium's personal point of view, for it was surely an attempt to reaffirm his ritual supremacy which had been threatened by John and Thomas who had ignored him to consult David/*Kafudzi*.

Andrew, it will be remembered, was village headman of Tatenda village and also the spirit-medium recognised as supreme in the village. His authority in the village undoubtedly rested more on his status as medium than as headman, because his headmanship had been more nominal than real. Andrew was an ineffectual sort of person in everyday life, and he relied on his spirit-mediumship for whatever respect he had in the village. That John and Thomas could ignore him in this instance in order to consult another medium was surely a serious threat to his authority.

This seance was, in fact, an important turning point in the development of events in Tatenda. Andrew, by responding to what he saw as a threat from John's quarter, found himself automatically aligned with James. Later on, when Thomas himself began to go into trance and to claim spiritual seniority over Andrew/*Mavu*, the coalition between James and Andrew became the stronger.

Thomas and David/*Kafudzi*

Soon after John's arrival at David's village, David/*Kafudzi* noticed Thomas's troubles, and pointed out that their resolution was bound up with that of John. Only by resolving Thomas's plight could John hope to get better. David/*Kafudzi* divined that Thomas's allergies were due to two factors. In the first place there was a spirit or spirits wanting to 'come out' and make him its (their) host, and in the second place somebody, who was motivated to prevent this happening, had used *futa*, a medicine (*muti*) designed to prevent possession. When the two forces of the spirit and the *futa* meet within the chosen host's body, then, it is believed, serious illness or death ensue due to the battle going on inside him.

Both Thomas and John agreed to let David/*Kafudzi* perform the ritual necessary to remove the effects of the *futa* and to bring Thomas into full medium status. This having been agreed, Thomas spent as much time as he could spare from his teaching in David/*Kafudzi*'s village and was soon incorporated into the society of the other neophyte mediums, even becoming David/*Kafudzi*'s favourite. After a series of rituals consisting mainly of prolonged dancing and lustrations in the nearby river, Thomas went into trance, possessed by a spirit of the same spirit lineage (Vatsunga) as one of David's other spirits. The Vatsunga are a lineage of hero spirits linked to the Nyandoro clan to which Thomas's mother belonged. David/*Kafudzi* told Thomas that he would also act as host to a further two spirits, one of the same spirit lineage as *Kafudzi*, and the other an ancestor spirit (*mudzimu*) senior to that which currently possessed his half-sister Ruth. This would make Thomas potentially the most senior medium in Tatenda village (see genealogy 2, p. 74/5).

David/*Kafudzi* had succeeded in bringing about an improvement in Thomas's condition where others had failed, a significant event from various points of view.

Firstly, David appreciated Thomas's youth, intelligence and education, and saw in him a worthy disciple. David's mission to encourage a new faith in the ancestors and in 'traditional' practice required the help of young and influential men and women and he no doubt saw in Thomas such a person.

I can only surmise that Thomas accepted David/*Kafudzi*'s analysis of the situation both because it tallied with his views about the rest of Tatenda village and his personal ambitions. Thomas was as impressed as most people by David's powerful personality and performance in trance; he sympathised with his methods and aims and may have seen the advantages of allying himself to such a dynamic 'master'.

From the point of view of John and Thomas in relation to the rest of Tatenda village, David/*Kafudzi*'s divination in terms of James' use of *futa* was acceptable and accepted. An accusation of the use of *futa* to impede spirit-possession is, as was shown in chapter 2, an accusation of dangerous egoism. If James had been manipulating his position as eldest brother in economic terms by diverting the marriage payments for Carmen and the cash from the destocked cattle to his own ends, he was probably also operating in the same way by mystical means. Furthermore John was convinced that James had every reason to impede Thomas's mediumship, because he believed that James was afraid lest Thomas in trance expose his immoral behaviour to the rest of the village. From this time onwards both John and Thomas put their faith in Thomas's mediumship. They hoped that once established as an important high-level medium under the aegis of David/*Kafudzi*, Thomas would be able to assume sufficient ritual authority in Tatenda village to denounce James and bring about a suitable reparation. The three principal actors in this drama, David, John and Thomas, had their own very good reasons for ensuring that Thomas be rapidly and efficiently installed as a respected spirit-medium.

During the months of April, May and June, Thomas spent much of his spare time with John and David, looking after his brother and undergoing ritual treatment. As is the case with spirit-mediums, this did not involve the use of a complex pharmacopoeia, but rather the use of snuff (*bute*), water and embers. In addition, David/*Kafudzi* occasionally spent time with John, laying on hands or performing other seemingly *ad hoc* rituals. At first there was little improvement, and John began to have doubts as to whether he should not perhaps have gone to hospital. He asked David/*Kafudzi* if he would object if he were to go in for a medical inspection. David/*Kafudzi* replied that he would not mind, but the tenor of his reply left little doubt that it would not be advisable. John compromised

85

and, one day when David was away with most of his followers, the medical orderly from the Mahusekwa government clinic, with whom he had studied at Harare African hospital in Salisbury, was smuggled in to give four penicillin injections. It is doubtful whether they could have had any effect, for they resulted in no immediate improvement in John's condition.

However, as time went on, John gradually began to regain the use of his legs. Slowly he was able to walk, at first with the aid of friends, and later, on his own with sticks. By the end of May he could walk alone. It is difficult to put into words the effect that this cure had both on John and those who had spent so much time with him. At the onset of the illness both he, myself and many others feared for his life. Yet now he was walking again, apparently totally cured. A 'miracle' had taken place and it was not long before the news spread around. More and more patients flocked to consult David/*Kafudzi* and John seemed quite willing to be put on display whenever it was necessary. By the end of June he was able to return to work.

John now felt himself wholly vindicated in his initial insistence that his was an 'African illness'. Furthermore, because the cure had been effected on the divination that the illness had been caused by James, his suspicions were confirmed and his hostility exacerbated. Now that he was better he was able to turn his attention back to affairs in the village.

Towards the end of June 1965 both Thomas and John visited Tatenda village on the instructions of David/*Kafudzi*. Their plan was to hold a seance at the village during which Thomas would become possessed and explain to the village the reasons for John's illness. John claimed that Andrew/*Mavu* had been reluctant to tell the 'truth' lest this should bring about open conflict in the village. As Thomas's spirit was not of the same lineage 'it' would have no qualms in telling the Tatenda people the 'truth'. Only an outsider (*mutorwa*) could bring matters to a head.

At the seance which was held in Andrew's house, both Andrew and Thomas went into trance, the former as *Mavu*, the latter as *Pasipamire*. Thomas/*Pasipamire* began by announcing that he had some important things to say, but Andrew/*Mavu* rejoined by saying that as no-one in the village knew who Thomas's spirit really was, he had no right to speak. Until the identity of the new spirit had been disclosed and confirmed Thomas could say nothing. Thomas/*Pasipamire* refused to humble himself and remained quiet. Andrew/*Mavu* reacted with violence. 'You are no *mudzimu*', he shouted, 'you are *ngozi*' (dangerous aggrieved spirit). He went on to warn the people of Tatenda that this *ngozi*[6] was so dangerous that the whole village was in peril and that people approached Thomas's and John's houses at their own risk. He continued in like vein for some time and then roundly denounced David/*Kafudzi* also. He claimed that *Kafudzi* was not a reputable spirit but evil also and that by following his instructions Thomas and John were not only running the risk of harming themselves but the whole village. Then, to make his point even more forcefully, Andrew/*Mavu* launched a physical attack on Thomas/*Pasipamire*. In the struggle that ensued, he broke a sword-stick and a wooden plate which Thomas had borrowed for the occasion from David/*Kafudzi*.

After this débâcle Thomas and John left Tatenda and did not return until *kurova guva*, the second funeral rite, for their father. John did, however, leave his wife to stay in the village, but she spent many unhappy weeks due to the boycott that Andrew/*Mavu* had imposed.

On learning of the events at the seance, David/*Kafudzi* explained that the incident had arisen because Andrew had been feigning trance. He had used this as a pretext for launching his violent attack on Thomas whom he had in fact wanted to kill lest he succeed in establishing ritual supremacy in the village.

These events provide an example of something which has been stressed throughout this book, namely that there are a number of possible explanations for any one event and that that which is accepted by any one person or group of persons is generally the one which is most acceptable to them. Andrew's words and actions were not only in accord with his own personal fears for his ritual supremacy in the village; they were also likely to command the support of James and his supporters. Andrew's struggle against Thomas for ritual supremacy had become inextricably linked to the more mundane dispute between James and John. The political rift in Tatenda village had resulted in a religious one also.

But what is particularly interesting about these events is the precarious nature of the authority of the spirit-mediums concerned, for their pronouncements in trance were only accepted by those for whom they were politically acceptable.

John and Thomas were unable to accept the words and actions of Andrew/ *Mavu* for obvious reasons. Because they had already in the past recognised Andrew as a genuine spirit-medium they could not question his fundamental genuineness but could denounce his behaviour on that occasion by assuming him to have temporarily feigned trance.

Andrew and the other people in the village however had never recognised Thomas's mediumship so they were able to denounce him in far stronger terms by claiming that his spirit was dangerous to them all. Andrew was successful in this denunciation because the majority of the people in the village either through inertia or for other reasons (James, during his period as a rich man had dealt out many favours in the village) were in favour of the *ancien régime* and were reluctant to accept a new and unproven tribal authority.

But perhaps of greater interest than the denunciation of Thomas was the denunciation of David/*Kafudzi*, for it might be expected that Andrew, who was a mere low-level medium, would not be able to challenge such an exalted authority. However, at this time David/*Kafudzi* was still only beginning his career as a spirit-medium and although he had already had considerable success and built up quite a large sphere of influence, his reputation had not yet reached the locality of the village of Tatenda. Because of this, Andrew was able not only to ignore him, but to go as far as to denounce him as the medium of an evil spirit. It was the observations of these, and later events, which led me to perceive that spirit-mediums in Chiota are not unquestioned authorities. Their status as spirit-mediums is valid only within their spheres of influence, and even then, as John and Thomas's attitude to Andrew shows, they must still issue acceptable statements in order to be accepted as genuine.

In their attempt to establish ritual supremacy in Tatenda village, John and Thomas had suffered a severe set-back. But they were not prepared to give in and their continued hopes of being able to achieve this prominence in the village was one of the reasons for their now going to consult a different high-level medium, Edward/*Chigara*.

Thomas alters his allegiances

Edward/*Chigara* (see Genealogy 2) was perhaps the most widely respected medium in Chiota Tribal Trust Land at that time. *Chigara* was a well-established hero spirit who had a long succession of mediums and was considered 'son' to *Biri na Ganyiri* the senior hero spirit (*gombwe*) of the Nyandoro clan. Apart from this medium's generalised fame, he was also specifically linked to the people of Tatenda; Andrew's wife (E13) was a member of the Nyandoro clan as was his brother-in-law Matibini, and it had been through these affines that Andrew was presented at Edward's seance house (*banya*); Thomas's mother (D9) was also a member of the Nyandoro clan and his father's sister's son, Choto, lived close by Edward's *banya* and had close social relations with him.

For these reasons it was not difficult for Thomas to be introduced to Edward/ *Chigara* as the new medium of *Pasipamire* of the same spirit lineage (Vatsunga) as *Chigara* himself. Edward/*Chigara* acknowledged that Thomas was in fact the medium of *Pasipamire* but insisted that the mediumship could only be ratified under his tutelage. He was not prepared to recognise David/*Kafudzi*'s authority in this respect, and said that only he could direct the culminating rite of *kudya muropa* (see above, p. 32).

Thomas's passage from the patronage of David/*Kafudzi* was significant in the context of Tatenda village politics because both John and Thomas hoped that the backing of a spirit-medium who was recognised in the village might prove sufficient to sway the ritual balance in their favour. But it also had significance in relation to the power politics of the high-level mediums, because it affected relations between David/*Kafudzi* and Edward/*Chigara*.

David/*Kafudzi*'s rapid rise to fame had posed a threat to the already established mediums of Chiota, not least Edward/*Chigara*, for although Edward was host to a long established and well-proven spirit, David Mudiwa through his own efforts had carved out for himself a large following. Already there had been contact between the two mediums when David held a ritual (*bira*) to open his new seance house. On that occasion he sent messengers to visit Edward and to invite him as host of *Chigara* to attend the opening ritual. Edward/*Chigara* reacted with disdain. He had learned that one of David Mudiwa's possessing spirits was of the same spirit lineage as himself but that he had never been consulted on the matter. How could he attend a ritual at David's seance house when he, as senior medium had not yet received homage? He sent the messengers back and declined the invitation in a deliberate move to assert his threatened authority.

By accepting the tutelage of Thomas and thus wresting him from David's patronage he was able to inflict another blow to David's prestige. Indeed the reaction of David/*Kafudzi* was not of the calmest although he was powerless to bring Thomas back.

But this switch of patrons was also of significance to Thomas who could now boast of the ritual support of the two most popular high-level mediums in Chiota.

But before Thomas could be put through the final initiation rite of *kudya muropa*, further events were to precipitate new developments in Tatenda village.

Disaster strikes James' family

On 29 June 1965 I learned from Thomas that there had been three deaths in Tatenda. James had lost the youngest son of his first wife, his newly married second wife had lost her first born child in childbirth and his eldest daughter, Violet, had lost her two-year-old boy. All these deaths had occurred within two weeks.

Following a death it is customary for close kin to divine for its causes. I did not speak to James about the result of *gata* (divination into the causes of death) because it is kept secret anyway, and because of my association with John. However, others had their own views.

John's wife said that she had been confided in by James' first wife. There was a reason for this, for both women were in a sense drawn together by their respective predicaments. James' first wife had suffered from the arrival of James' new wife; she felt herself ignored by her husband and was afraid of losing many of his favours. John's wife, for her part, suffered from being to a large extent ostracised in the village due to the widely held belief that John's association with David/*Kafudzi* was causing the rest of the family to suffer. James' wife told John's that people were saying that John had caused the death of the children. She did not specify the means but implied that David/*Kafudzi* had been able to cure John in exchange for the lives of other members of the lineage. She added that others believed that the deaths were caused by her own mother, who had misused her *mombe yo amai* (see below, p. 99) and had therefore angered the children's matrilineal female ancestors who are responsible for life and death.

Mideas, the son of Christopher's sister, said that he thought the deaths could have been caused by John's mother in retaliation for her own death at the hand of James' mother.

Mashoshera, husband of one of Moses' sisters, said he thought that the whole trouble was due to the anger of the lineage ancestors because Rufu's spirit had not yet been brought back into the lineage as a fully fledged *mudzimu* at *kurova guva*.

Spirits of protest

A nearby village headman, who had very little contact with Tatenda village thought that the deaths were due to James' misuse of medicines (*muti*), which he had used to build up his business. It was well known that such medicines were dangerous and that if all their rules were not obeyed, they would turn back on their owner (see above, p. 24). This interpretation was also favoured by John and Thomas.

They obtained their own information from Thomas's spirit, and were able to reject James' suspicions by saying that he had not consulted a spirit-medium but a *nganga*. They invoked the belief that whereas a spirit-medium is totally honest, *ngangas* can never be trusted, as they deal also in magic and witchcraft.

In this further example of multiple explanation of misfortune, each interpretation is consistent with the interests of the interpreter. James chooses to believe in the guilt of John, while John believes that James has brought the trouble on himself by using medicines (*miti*) for his business.

But whatever the specific reasons for the calamities might be, James shared a common view that a prior condition for bringing an end to them was to hold the second funeral rite, *kurova guva* for Rufu. The belief that much of the trouble had resulted from the fact that Rufu's spirit had not yet been 'brought back' was another way of saying that village affairs could only be resolved, for better or for worse, once the problem of Rufu's inheritance had been settled.

Kurova guva

On 3 July, Thomas told me that he had had word from John's wife that she had seen the other women of the village preparing beer for *kurova guva* on the instructions of Andrew, James, Moses and Manyuchi. Furious that this action had been taken without his having been informed he telephoned to John in Salisbury. John decided that although it was despicable that James should take such action without consulting them or even letting them know, they would nevertheless participate. He gave orders that his wife was to prepare her own beer. At *kurova guva* there are three main brews of beer. The major is brewed by all the women present and is used for all visitors and the three ritual pots of *murongedzo*, *dziva* and *mumvuri*. It is called 'the great beer' (*hwahwa hwe guru*). In addition there is special beer brewed for the mother's brothers of the dead man (*hwahwa hwe madzisekuru*) and each domestic group prepares its own beer, the 'little beer' (*hwahwa hwe diki*), which it uses for its own private guests. In Tatenda village 'little beer' was brewed independently by James' mother, James' wives, Chipanda, Andrew's wives, Christopher's mother, Christopher's wife, the wife of Moses and Manyuchi's sister and mother. Now John's wife was to prepare hers, but as she was not officially informed she was a day late in starting.

On Friday 9 July I went with Thomas to Tatenda. We found the 'great beer' being given its final mixing, but no beer was officially drunk as proceedings had not officially started. Indeed there were hardly any men there, only ourselves,

90

Spirit-mediums in ritual action

Chipanda (senior *musukuru*, known in this context as *derwe*) and Manyuchi. James, Andrew, Moses and John were absent. Thomas began to wonder whether James was staying away on purpose now that he knew John would be present.

Nothing could be started until a *nganga* had been visited to 'divine for the beer' – i.e. to make sure that the beer had been properly prepared and that the ritual would be effective.

As James and Andrew should be a part of this ceremony, Thomas and I were sent to find them. They were at James' shop in Nyandoro, making bricks for James. They both denied that it was their responsibility to divine for this beer, saying that it was the duty of Naison and Moses, the former because of his appointment as regent, the latter because he was the eldest male agnate in Tatenda. We returned to the village after James and Andrew had agreed to follow on Sunday morning. In fact they appeared on that same day, but there were still very few people in the village. John had arrived, as had his sister Carmen and her husband and his sisters, Augustine from school in Goromonzi, and Herbert. John was angry at the lack of organisation, complaining that as James and Andrew had set everything in motion, they could at least see it through.

On the evening of Saturday 10 July, Chibwe, the senior *sekuru* (mother's brother) present, distributed the first beer (*musumo*), formally announcing to those present that work had begun (*kuzarurwa kwe basa*). The whole night was spent in dancing in Christopher's house, and in the morning all gathered outside for the journey to the grave of Rufu to 'bring back the spirit' (*kutora mudzimu*). It is a rule that this visit to the grave should take place before the sun rises, however, on this occasion it got lighter and lighter without any sign of movement. This was largely because Naison, who was supposed to be in charge, was hopelessly drunk, but also because Moses, who was also responsible, had not yet appeared from his own house where he had gone to sleep. Ultimately the procession set off, with the wife of Christopher and another *muroora* (daughter-in-law of Rufu) carrying beer. Moses and the husband of Mandifusa (E19), Rufu's eldest daughter, approached the grave, and the latter threw a stone at it, after which the beer which had been carried was drunk. Thomas remained quite distant from the beer and the grave, and the people. As the beer was being drunk, Moses was frantically yelling and exhorting everybody to be quick about it and to get it all finished before the sun came up. This done, we returned to the village.

Thomas and John had observed this irreverent display with anguish. In the first place the ritual had been rushed, and secondly, the business at the grave had not conformed to general practice, which is for the *vatukwa* (wives of mother's brothers and sister's sons) of the dead man to laugh and joke, beating the grave (*kurova guva*) with branches, and for beer to be smeared on the grave. Thomas said that he thought it had been done wrongly to bring further misfortune on the village. (*Kuchapinda mhepo mu musha* – there shall enter a great wind (meaning trouble) into the village). Both Thomas and John blamed Moses for this, saying that it was not really Naison's fault because he was not entirely *compos mentis*.

91

Spirits of protest

After *kutora mudzimu*, the pot of beer known as *mumvuri* ('in the shadow') was drunk and an ox provided by the husband of the senior daughter (i.e. of Mandifusa) was slaughtered for relish. Even the distribution of the meat was confused, and during the subsequent food and drink, an argument developed between Andrew and Chakanyuka, a son of Rowesa, which came to blows; a bad omen at such a ceremony. Andrew apologised and said that he had never fought anyone in his life before.

After the drinking of the two pots of beer called *murongedzo* (from *kurongendza*, to point out) and *dziva*, (pool), the day passed with drinking and conversation.

During the night, John told me that he had conversed with Andrew and Simon, the eldest son of Tatenda who had arrived from his farm in Mount Darwin, about the events of the following day, i.e. the matter of succession to property and the settling of Rufu's debts and credits. Both Andrew and Simon had pleaded with him not to cause an open breach and to let the matter drop, but John had raised other grievances such as the way in which Andrew, in trance, had attacked Thomas at the seance in the previous month. Andrew, consistently with the Zezuru theory of spirit-possession, denied all knowledge of the incident and said that the reason for the boycott of John's family was to be found with the other brothers Christopher, James, Manyuchi and Moses.

The following day Thomas and John planned what future action they should take. John was determined to expose James as the one who had squandered Rufu's estate, and to gain acknowledgement of the ways in which he had been so badly treated. He decided, however, to concentrate on the question of Carmen's bridewealth, as he had no legal argument as regards the inter-vivos transaction of the money from the destocked cattle. He would press James to give to him what was outstanding of Carmen's bridewealth which had been promised to him by Rufu when she had married.

In the afternoon all gathered outside the house of Christopher's mother, in which Rufu had died. Both of Rufu's wives agreed to be formally inherited by Rufu's heir. Rufu's walking stick (*tsvimbo*), symbol of his fatherhood of the family, was first passed to his sister, Rowesa, who then passed it to Mavis, the senior daughter present. She then handed it to Christopher who then passed it to James, who first refused, but then reluctantly accepted. He thus became Rufu's successor and took on the role of 'husband' to Rufu's old widows and father to his siblings.

After this, James took a seat beside a pot of beer and received small cash gifts from all those present who by so doing acknowledged officially his new status. It was a period of licence, and joking was permitted. John said, as he threw a shilling into the box: 'Well, James, I must say you are the biggest liar I have ever met!' This was met by a brave smile, for on the next day was to be settled the inheritance of Rufu's property, credits and debts.

After Thomas had read from his book what had been dictated by Rufu concerning the monies outstanding from his sons-in-law for their marriage payments, and after they had all agreed with this, John stood up to make his claims. He stressed that this was a public occasion at which the lineage had come together in order to be 'washed' (*kugezwa*) by non-lineage kinsmen, whom he referred to as *vatorwa* (outsiders). He therefore thought it right that he should press his claim to the bridewealth which had come from Carmen's husband, and was by rights his. One of the sister's sons said that James should reply as he was now 'father'. James said that he had no knowledge of what John had said, whereupon others stood up with their comments. Rowesa, Rufu's sister from Wedza said that it should all be forgotten. Manyuchi said that John had no right to claim this money when he had other full sisters anyway who were married. Besides, he added, how could John have acquired the wealth he had, without help from his father? John denied having had any help from his father and added with pride that he was not even in need of money. 'I have £200 in the bank. I am concerned with my rights only.'

It was clear that John's chances of wresting any concessions from James were minimal. Of those who rose to speak the majority were either in favour of James' position or advocated that the whole affair be forgotten. John and Thomas realised that they had been defeated and soon after the discussion they left the village.

Now that they had failed to have any effect on matters in Tatenda, and that James was their 'father' and so had moral authority over them, they decided amongst themselves that the only course open to them was to move out of Tatenda village either to another area in Chiota Tribal Trust Land or to a Native Purchase Area. Meanwhile, now that *kurova guva* was past, the ritual interdiction on the village had been lifted and John and Thomas turned their attentions once more to Thomas's mediumship.

Thomas's initiation

Edward/*Chigara* ordered John to arrange for this *bira* to take place at Tatenda. He, *Chigara*, would be present to supervise. However, as beer for such important rituals must be brewed by old women who have ceased to have sexual intercourse, John was thrown to the mercy of the mother of James and the mother of Christopher, the only two such qualified women in Tatenda. They pleaded that they were too old to brew the beer, thus making it impossible for the ritual to be held in the village itself. Thomas was disappointed. He would have liked to see the people of Tatenda witness the presence in their village of such an important medium as Edward, but a compromise was reached whereby the ritual would be held in Edward's seance house and the beer would be brewed by old women who lived nearby and who would be paid for their services.

Towards the end of September the beer was started and Thomas was enjoined by Edward/*Chigara* to refrain from sexual intercourse until all was over. However,

Thomas not only ignored the interdiction, but was found out by Edward/*Chigara* to have slept with his own mistress. The conflict which was generated between the two mediums was expressed and resolved between their respective 'spirits'. Thomas's version of the episode is as follows:

Thomas had a girlfriend who lived near Edward's village. They had exchanged love tokens and slept together. Edward also loved the girl and wanted to marry her, but as this went against the girl's wishes, she resolved to tell Edward of her love for Thomas. Edward was so angry that he rushed to the house of Veronica, Thomas's classificatory mother, and told her that *Pasipamire* had come to him in a dream and told him that his host, Thomas, had been having sexual relations with his, Edward's, girlfriend at at time when he was forbidden. Edward let Veronica know that this was a most serious offence and threatened to call off the ritual and to summon all the spirit-mediums in the Nyandoro area, and the chief as well, to sit in judgement. Veronica who was very fond of Thomas and who had helped him and his brother John throughout their difficulties sent word to Thomas as soon as she was able. Thomas then telephoned John in Salisbury who drove straight out and took Thomas to visit Edward who was found in his seance house in the company of Choto and his mother. According to Thomas, Edward feigned possession by *Chigara* and told him that he would have to pay a heavy fine of five head of cattle. If he refused to pay, then the case would have to be judged by all the spirit-mediums of Nyandoro and the chief. At this stage Edward's mother intervened and advised him against such a course of action, pointing out that it would then be public knowledge that Edward was sleeping with 'undesirable women'. Edward/*Chigara* then ordered Thomas out of the house, but at this moment Thomas went into trance, being possessed by his an-cestor spirit (as yet unidentified by name). Thomas's *mudzimu* then pleaded for compassion and suggested that his host (i.e. Thomas) should pay only £5 as an admission of guilt. Finally the two 'spirits' agreed amongst themselves that Thomas should pay a fine of £10 together with a cockerel and a goat.

Thomas told this story to emphasise two points. In the first place how good a negotiator his ancestor spirit was, and secondly what a trickster Edward really was. Thomas had heard from the girl how Edward had found out about his sex-ual activities and knew the story of the dream to be false. Furthermore, he sus-pected that Edward was not in trance during the discussion in his seance house and believed it to have been a ploy to make money. Wistfully he remembered that this sort of thing would never have happened with David/*Kafudzi* who had warned him of Edward's techniques for obtaining money. His mediumship was costing his brother John dearly for David/*Kafudzi* had already been presented with a cow in recognition of his services.

However John had no option but to pay up and the ritual duly began on 2 October 1965, marking the culmination of a long period of waiting. Present at the ritual were John, Thomas, their sisters Carmen and Filda, their mother's younger sister Veronica and two of her daughters, Choto and a few of his rela-

tives and the schoolboy son of Andrew. They had been to Tatenda village by car
in order to fetch people to the ritual, but although they all knew about it and
had been invited, James had gone to Salisbury, Andrew to Marandellas,
Christopher was not to be seen and Moses and Manyuchi said they were too ill to
travel. In spite of the fact that Thomas was now being recognised and sponsored
by Edward, a medium whom they all respected, they were still not prepared to
attend the ritual and so manifest their own recognition of Thomas's new status.

When they came back from Tatenda village they managed to squeeze one of
John's small black calves into the boot of the car. This was removed and allowed
to graze until such time as it would be sacrificed.

The *bira* took place on the night of Sunday 3 October. There were four pots
of beer, one for the mediums, one for the people of Nyandoro, one for the musicians and one for John's folk. The mediums remained in trance throughout the
night while others danced. Just before dawn, Choto and Tendai, the son of John's
sister Anna, washed their hands, tied the black calf to a tree and slit its throat.
This duty should have been performed by John's sons-in-law (*vakwasha*) but as
these were absent it was entrusted to sisters' sons (*vazukuru*). As soon as the calf
was dead, they reported to the *banya* that the beast had been killed, and the procession emerged; in the lead were the *mbira* players playing one of the most
famous tunes, Nyamaropa. They were followed by Edward/*Chigara* and Thomas/
Pasipamire both swathed in black cloths, wearing headdresses of ostrich plumes
(*ngundu*), and carrying their ritual staffs (*tsvimbo*) in their hands. After them
came two other mediums in trance, one Zhava and the daughter of Choto. Both
were possessed by *vadzimu*. Edward/*Chigara* put his mouth to the split in the
animal's neck and started to suck blood, after which it was Thomas/*Pasipamire*'s
turn. He lapped up the blood voraciously from a wooden bowl, which was then
handed by the mother of Edward to Zhava who refused it and then to Choto's
daughter, who drank lustily. Meanwhile Thomas/*Pasipamire*, aided by Edward/
Chigara, was helping himself to the raw liver (*chiropa*) and breast flesh of the
animal with the aid of a knife. All this took place in an atmosphere of considerable jubilation, with the women ululating and the men clapping their hands.
There were even some remarks to the effect that if the spirits were allowed to go
on much longer there would be no meat left for anyone else to eat, cooked, with
their *sadza*.

After this, the mediums washed their hands and returned to the *banya*, where
the spirit of Choto's daughter was reprimanded by Edward/*Chigara* for accepting
the blood. Apparently he should not have done so.

The rest of the day was spent by non-mediums in drinking and resting. The
mediums, for their part, remained inside the *banya*, always in trance, conversing
and sleeping. Thomas had taken two days off from school for the ritual and was
expected to be in trance until the Tuesday. All the meat from the ox was taken
by Edward/*Chigara* and dished out to the women of John's family for the various
meals.

95

During this period Thomas/*Pasipamire* made the momentous pronouncement that he wanted his *banya* to be built away from the village of Tatenda, in order to escape the effects of the 'witches' who lived there. He did not specify a site, but said that he would prefer it to be situated on the banks of a river which runs along the southern boundary of Chiota Reserve.

Thus was Thomas initiated as a new spirit-medium, 'proven' genuine by the ritual eating of raw blood under the auspices of one of the most widely respected high-level mediums of the district, Edward/*Chigara*.

However, a substantial part of Tatenda village had not attended the ritual. Their excuses were interpreted by John and Thomas as voluntary refusals which indicated that they were as yet not prepared to recognize Thomas's new status. Amongst the Zezuru it is as important to know who is absent from rituals as who is present, for presence generally signifies co-operation while absence implies hostility. What is important about these absences is that they were still able to ignore Thomas in spite of the fact that he now had the backing of Edward/*Chigara* who had direct ritual and kinship links with Andrew. I take this as evidence of the fact that even high-level mediums may be ignored if absolutely necessary and that Andrew, James and their faction, having won the day at *kurova guva*, felt themselves strong enough in the village to be able to refuse the invitation.

However, both Thomas and John had not yet given up all hope of gaining some ground in Tatenda and, when a *bira* ritual was organised in Tatenda to celebrate the new mediumship of Christopher, they resolved to attend, having been invited by Naison.

This time Thomas arrived with a new authority. He went into trance before either Christopher or Andrew or Matthew, who had also become a medium by this time, and John was there to act as his acolyte (*nechambo*), handing him his black cloth, symbol of his hero status and large black ostrich feather head-dress. However, in spite of this impressive performance, Thomas/*Pasipamire* was not able to make himself heard and the other mediums gave no recognition of his high status.

After this final failure both John and Thomas resolved to accept the advice of Thomas/*Pasipamire* and look for a suitable site for building a seance house. They visited a chief who agreed to let them build and farm in an uninhabited area on the banks of a river. This was the first of the 'miracles' that were to occur as proof of Thomas' calling, for, according to Thomas, the chief had indicated exactly the site that Thomas/*Pasipamire* had indicated earlier.

Towards the end of December, John broke the roof of his kitchen in Tatenda village and moved to live at the new site where he had had built two kitchens, one for his wife and the other for Thomas's and a simple meeting house. From this time onwards Thomas continued as a teacher, staying in the school during the week and received clients as a spirit-medium at the weekends. In fact the distinction between these roles was not entirely congruent with locality, for even in his school house he received clients and held seances.

After these events, my contacts with Thomas, John and Tatenda village became less frequent so I can only sketch in subsequent events up to the end of
1966.

Aftermath

Thomas continued to teach, but as time went on his reputation as a spirit-
medium waxed, and stories began to circulate about his triumphs, one of which
is of special interest.

During January of 1966 there had been a prolonged period of drought which
affected not only the farmers in Chiota, but also the European farmers on its
periphery. One of these, whose nickname was Chimusoro (big-head) sent a depu-
tation of labourers to visit Thomas/*Pasipamire* to see what he could do about the
situation. The medium told the labourers that by the time they had returned
home rain would have fallen. It did, and a few days later the labourers returned
with a gift of £2 from the farmer. Thomas told me that Thomas/*Pasipamire* had
refused the gift and had told the labourers that they should take the money, and
instead of spending their day off dancing for him as they had been instructed by
Chimusoro, they should use the cash to buy themselves beer and enjoy themselves at Chimusoro's expense![7]

After the initiation rite at Edward's seance house, Thomas restored good relations with David/*Kafudzi*, on whom he continued to model himself. His reputation as a diviner, as an exorciser of witchcraft and as a healer grew and he was
very much in demand at rituals held in villages nearby and even further afield. He
also established firm relations with a nearby chief who occasionally hired out his
car and himself as driver when Thomas needed to travel. According to rumour,
Thomas/*Pasipamire* took on the role of chief's adviser, and it is interesting to
speculate to what extent he had thus superseded the incumbent senior high-level
medium in the chiefdom.

On the domestic front, Thomas continued to act as oracle for John and the
small group of people who had gathered around as followers. No important decisions were made without prior consultation with Thomas/*Pasipamire*, and, now
that both John and Thomas were isolated from social pressures from their
brothers in Tatenda, Thomas was able to divorce his wife, whom he had never
wanted to marry, on the orders of Thomas/*Pasipamire*!

John continued in good health working in Salisbury and he and his full siblings found a welcome solidarity around the focus of their brother medium.

Back in Tatenda, James' affairs went from bad to worse and he had to close
his large shop in Wedza, transferring what stock remained to the smaller one in
Nyandoro. But it was of no avail, and after a number of thefts business became
so bad that this shop too had to be closed. Rumour had it that James, in desper-
ation, had tried to kill a small girl in order that his business medicine might
function and draw some of the misfortune away from him. Two friends of James

97

had been found trying to murder the girl and according to one rumour they had been paid £4 each for their services. Thomas/*Pasipamire* claimed that James' continuing ill-fortune was the work of *Pasipamire* who was punishing him for having ignored him in the past. Only by coming to beg forgiveness would he be able to escape this mystical persecution.

In sum, the net result of the crisis was that John and Thomas had declared their independence from the rest of the village and, under the guidance of Thomas/*Pasipamire* had established a new and thriving village nucleus of their own. Thomas had solved his own vocational problem and was now quite well established as a prominent spirit-medium. James had maintained his position as head of the family, but his fortunes didn't improve. When I left Rhodesia towards the end of 1966 harmony had not returned to Tatenda village, for not only had James' new poverty brought about a number of problems for his wives, mother and brothers, but the animosities that had been stirred up had not died down. Indeed, when Phineas, the son of Rufu's sister, died, his close kin believed the death to have been caused by James' sorcery and in order to avoid further attacks they moved their houses some distance from the village.

Analysis

The Political factor in the explanation of misfortune

There is sufficient evidence in these events to demonstrate quite clearly the tenuous relationship between physical symptoms and their explanation. In all the cases cited the explanation accepted by a given person as 'correct' was that which most made sense in political terms. For this reason any one misfortune usually carried many different explanations. Even in the case of Thomas's allergies, which are generally agreed to herald spirit-mediumship, there was no consensus as to the *type* of spirit. Through all developments James chose to explain matters by putting the blame on John and vice versa, for the village was dominated by the cleavage between these two persons. Thus, while James saw John as being responsible for the deaths in his family, John put the blame on James and his use of business medicine; while Thomas's enormous difficulties in becoming a spirit-medium were interpreted by John as being due to James' having tried to thwart the possession by the use of *futa* medicine, James accepted Andrew's interpretation that the spirit involved was itself dangerous.

In the last analysis this dominant cleavage overran all other kinds of explanation which might have been acceptable in other circumstances. Thus the suggestion that John's sickness might have been caused by his wife's use of love medicine (*mufuwhira*) might have been accepted had it not been that all persons involved preferred to explain it in terms of James' jealousy. John's sister would have been satisfied to blame the love medicine were her loyalty to John not stronger than her animosity towards his wife.

98

But the dispute between James and John was not simply the result of a clash of personalities. They were brought into conflict because of their structural relationship as senior sons of different mothers in a polygonous household. As has already been suggested in chapter 2, the clash between narrow matrisegment interests and wider lineage loyalties is a feature of Zezuru society and often results in tension and conflict. This is especially likely in lineages which do not have rights in chiefly office, as is the case in Tatenda village. Where there is not interest in office, the centripetal forces running along agnatic lines give way to the centrifugal ones generated in matrisegments.

It is quite clear from the case in Tatenda village that children are firmly identified with their mothers and vice versa. John stated quite explicitly that his mother's death had prejudiced his relations with his father and his brother-in-law went so far as to suggest that James' mother had killed John's by witchcraft in order that she and her 'house' (*imba*) might dominate in the family. I have already pointed out the symbolic and instrumental role of wives and mothers as points of division within partilineage, but the affair of Carmen's bridewealth provides further evidence for this.

The rules concerning the allocation of bridewealth are somewhat confused, due to the opposing ideals of lineage solidarity on the one side and matrisegment solidarity on the other. It is sometimes held that a father must use the bridewealth that accrues on the marriage of his daughters to finance the first marriages of his sons regardless of their maternal affiliation. John, however, put forward the view that the bridewealth that a daughter 'earned' should be earmarked for the financing of her full brothers' marriages and that at least as far as bridewealth was concerned, the finances of each matri-segment should be kept separate. It is interesting that James did not choose to challenge this principle; he merely affirmed that John had been given the bridewealth necessary for his marriage. Others who contributed to the discussion, however, felt that John was wrong to put forward matrisegment interests since they were all the sons of the same father.

A further indication of the wifely threat to lineage solidarity is to be found in the institution of the 'cow of the mother' (*mombe yo amai*) which entered peripherally in the case at Tatenda. When a woman marries, her husband is obliged to present her with a cow which is a gift to her and to her matrilineal ancestresses and which is supposed to guarantee the health and wellbeing of any children that are borne. This cow, although owned by the married woman may not be killed. She may dispose of its progeny, but only with the permission of her brothers, that is of her natal lineage. The *mombe yo amai* is at once a symbol of a wife's distinctive affiliation in the lineage to which she has been married, but it may also be instrumental in establishing independence of herself and her children. In other villages it was not uncommon to find a woman possessing a large number of cattle which had been generated from the initial cow and which she could use (always with the permission of her brothers, of course), to convert into cash

99

either to buy things for herself or for her children. By such means a woman could attain a certain economic power over her children and thus diminish paternal authority.

The women that Rufu married provided children for him and for his lineage; they all had the clan name of Shave and the praise name of Museyamwa. And yet the children were differentiated within the lineage with reference to these very women who gave to them their distinctive matrilateral affiliations. Each group of Rufu's children possessed a different circle of kin they could not marry, and were involved in the affairs of different mother's brothers. At the same time these different groups of children were raised separately by their mothers so that the social exchanges with which they were involved during childhood were restricted more or less to their relations between themselves and with their mothers who were seen as the sole providers of their sustenance. The mutual obligations that developed within these matrifocal cells were sufficiently strong and binding to threaten the wider lineage loyalties which are one of the strongest ideals of Zezuru society. Interestingly enough, the cycle had already begun to repeat itself. Carmen was hostile to John's wife and expressed this in her suspicion that she had administered love medicine to her husband. She resented the fact that John was no longer only her brother, but someone else's husband. She felt that John's wife was luring him away, both economically and emotionally from his attachment to herself and her other siblings.

But amongst the Zezuru of Chiota, rivalries between agnates not only find an outlet in mutual accusations of witchcraft and sorcery but also in the competition for the mediumship of their common ancestors.

The spirit-mediums of Tatenda village

Up until the death of Rufu there had been three spirit-mediums amongst Mutero's descendants, Margaret, the daughter of Tatenda, by his first wife, Andrew, the son of Tatende by his second wife and Ruth who was the daughter of Rufu by his first wife. Ruth lived out of Tatenda village and practised as a herbalist/diviner while Margaret, who was a widow, lived with her brother Manyuchi but both these mediums acknowledged that Andrew was the senior one of the village, in spite of the fact that his possessing ancestor spirit was geneaologically junior to that possessing Ruth.

However, with the death of Rufu and the resultant strivings between the various sections of the family, a number of new mediums appeared. Not only did John's matrisegment produce Thomas as a medium, but Christopher, Rufu's son by his second wife, and Matthew, son of Mamire also became spirit-mediums. The political tribulations within the lineage were accompanied by a proliferation of spirit-mediums, one of whom, Thomas, actually challenged the overall authority of Andrew.

The reasons are not hard to find once it is remembered that spirit-mediums are only accepted if their pronouncements are acceptable. In the situation of conflict that developed out of Rufu's death, Andrew was no longer able to pronounce to the satisfaction of all the people of Tatenda. The breakdown of consensus into two factions led to the emergence of two spirit-mediums each acting as oracle of one of them, and each one being rejected as 'false' by his political opponents. Each faction established its own direct line of ancestral pronouncements.

Such a situation of almost open conflict for mediumship goes contrary to the belief that it is the spirits who choose their hosts and that these latter act purely as mouthpieces. When asked why people seemed so keen to thwart spirit-mediumship in rival segments and to encourage it in their own when the identity of the host of a particular spirit is theoretically irrelevant, they replied that it wasn't that they could actually control the ancestors, but that mediumship 'conferred' on a person implied moral worth and was therefore a matter of pride. The belief that ancestors choose their hosts on the strength of their moral qualities (*hana*) (see above p. 36) served to justify competition for mediumship.

Once again, the proliferation of spirit-mediums amongst the various segments of Mutero's lineage and the ritual independence which this gave them was not peculiar to Tatenda village. The same thing happens generally and at other levels of social structure. Mutero's lineage was only of small depth and span, due to the fact that Mutero was a stranger to Nenguo's chieftaincy and to the fact that his descendants had no rights in chiefly office. But in larger royal lineages, whose members do have rights in chiefly office and who therefore retain political links, competition for mediumship of crucial ancestors and for ritual dominance takes place between larger lineage segments. Segments of royal lineages (*imba*) about which chiefly office rotates, tend to compete with one another for ancestral favour through the competition for mediumship. In sum, the ritual rivalry in Tatenda village is a structural feature of Zezuru society and is to be found at all levels of social structure.

But, returning to the specific case of Tatenda village, the emergence of Thomas as a medium was not only an assertion of ritual independence of John's matrisegment; it was part of an elaborate strategy to establish ritual and political dominance in the village. By considering the nature of this strategy and by assessing its effectiveness, it will be possible to say something more about the sociology of spirit-mediumship.

John's strategy

First, what were John's grievances and what were his goals? His grievances have been spelt out in some detail already and were in essence that he had been denied his full rights as Rufu's son due to the misuse of family funds by his half-brother James. His aims were to get back the money that he was owed, and, if possible, humiliate James thus punishing him for what John considered his errant behaviour. I don't think that John ever had any serious hope that he might be appointed Rufu's successor, but he certainly intended to establish a powerful position for himself in Tatenda village.

The strategy which he adopted was not, I think, carefully planned in all its details. It developed more or less spontaneously in response to other events, particularly the emergence of Thomas as a spirit-medium. John hoped that, by having Thomas initiated as a high-level medium, he would be able to expose publicly James' misdeeds and so not only wrest compensation from him, but also establish ritual supremacy in the village. These aims were made perfectly explicit in conversations between John and Thomas and Carmen at which I was present.

But this strategy failed, because the rest of the village continued to recognise Andrew/*Mavu* as their medium and accepted his announcement that Thomas was the medium of an aggrieved *ngozi* spirit. Why was this so? The answer, I think, lies in the fact that the rest of the village was so committed to the *ancien régime*, in its political, economic and religious aspects that it could or would not accept Thomas's claims to high-level spirit-mediumship.

James had been something of a rich man and undoubtedly one of the reasons for his decline as such was his generosity towards his kin. Whenever he visited the village he brought presents from the shop for his mother and others and when he required paid labour, for example for the making of bricks and building, he employed Andrew, Manyuchi and Mishek, as in fact he was doing shortly before Rufu's second funerary rite. Over the years he had established ties of indebtedness in the village which contributed to his strong political position. Although John felt that he had been excluded from this patronage, the rest of the village had benefited from it and James was therefore popular with them.

John's relation to the rest of the village was quite different. In the first place he was a professional man and therefore not in a position to hire labour, and secondly, his attitude to money was that it should be used not to buy conciliatory presents for needy villagers, who could be won over with even the smallest gifts, but to educate his younger siblings that they might be financially independent of him. He often told me of this policy and gave it as a reason for the fact that he had himself left school after doing only standard VI. He said that as eldest brother of a group of brothers and sisters with no mother, it was his duty to look after them all. Furthermore, by spending his money now to educate them he would be spared responsibility for them in later life.

In other words, while James adopted an economic policy designed to ensure his popularity in the whole village, John adopted one which was designed to enrich the matrisegment of which he was head. It is not difficult to see, then, why John failed in his attempt to wrest the outstanding bridewealth from James at Rufu's second funerary rite.

And this also explains, in my view, the reasons for John and Thomas's failure in the religious sphere. Andrew was one of the villagers most dependent on James' goodwill and at the same time was being threatened as the village's ritual authority by Thomas's pretensions. The rest of the village sided with James and Andrew and was thus obliged to accept Andrew/*Mavu*'s pronouncements which were an expression of political interests. Thomas/*Pasipamire* was not accepted by Andrew/*Mavu* and the villagers because his expected pronouncements (he never actually had the chance of saying what he thought) were unacceptable. Ritual authority is null unless it is believed in, and in this case Thomas was unable to make himself heard against the majority view. It might be possible to argue that John's strategy of trying to influence village affairs by ritual means was ingenuous because the political and economic situation was so heavily weighted against him.

But, even if John's attempts to assert himself in the village had failed, they nevertheless enabled him to cut his losses and move out of the village to form a new residential nucleus. Thomas/*Pasipamire* gave the order to build his seance house out of Tatenda village on the banks of the Mfuri river and John did not hesitate to accept. The dispute between Andrew/*Mavu* and Thomas/*Pasipamire* had enabled and indeed precipitated the fission between the two factions in the village much as witchcraft accusations do in other societies.

Linked with John's ambitions in the context of Tatenda village politics was Thomas's desire to become a high-level spirit-medium.

Thomas's rise as a spirit-medium

Although Thomas's entry into spirit-mediumship seemed at the time to be a serious set-back to my fieldwork, it put me in a privileged position to follow most of the developments in his progress and thus to gain relatively easy access to David/*Kafudzi* and Edward/*Chigara*. These developments may be considered in four stages, first the onset of affliction, second the divination of the cause of the affliction, third the rituals leading to official initiation into spirit-medium status and the removal of the symptoms and fourth, the establishment of his own seance house. Although the basic pattern was as I described it in chapter 3, Thomas's experience was particularly difficult due to the opposition in Tatenda village and the seniority of his possessing spirits.

The initial symptoms were especially harsh and brought considerable hardship to Thomas and those who cared for him. Not only were his normal activities severely curtailed, but also those of Anna, his sister, who was obliged to spend a considerable amount of time and energy in the preparation of his special diet.

The nature of Thomas's symptoms meant that all his social relationships were affected so that there could be little doubt of the metamosphosis which was occurring. During the zenith of these allergies, while Thomas was still my assistant but incapable of performing his duties, I resolved to try a very crude experiment. Taking him one day to Salisbury, I left him in the room of a colleague at the university who smoked as many cigarettes as he could with the windows closed. Thomas did not react. I was forced to the conclusion, therefore, that the allergies

could only be explained in terms of Thomas *in his social context*. That he could
no longer write or read was significant in informing people that he was no longer
a teacher, while the other allergies, in particular those to tobacco smoke and
petrol fumes, informed of his impending new status as a spirit-medium. My colleague could be expected neither to understand the significance of an allergy to
cigarette smoke, nor to be interested in it if he could.

The interesting aspect of the divination stage is that David/*Kafudzi*'s interpretation was accepted while that of Andrew/*Mavu* was not. Andrew/*Mavu* had
been non-specific in his divination and had suggested stalling tactics like buying
gifts for the spirit. These did not work, and only after coming into contact with
David/*Kafudzi* did Thomas (and John) accept his interpretation that Thomas was
to be host to three important spirits (two of them hero spirits). Although there
can be no certainty, I interpreted this fact in terms of John's having already committed himself to David/*Kafudzi*'s care, of John's political strategy in Tatenda
village, and of Thomas's growing conviction that he was to become a high-level
spirit-medium.

Thomas never admitted that he had a deliberate ambition to become a high-
level spirit-medium, for even if that is what he did want, to say so would have
been against the rules, which demand a manifest reluctance on the part of the
suffering neophyte. In spite of this 'official silence', however, I am confident in
inferring that Thomas felt a strong vocation towards spirit-mediumship which
was strengthened when he met David/*Kafudzi*.

I suggested earlier that Thomas's spirit-mediumship may have been in some
way connected with his having been my field assistant. Was it that through his
association with the ancestors and the past as mediated by David/*Kafudzi*, who,
as will be shown in the following chapter, was in the forefront of cultural
nationalism in Chiota, he was able to satisfy his own conscience which may have
suffered through his working with a white man, or, which is in many ways the
same thing, to convince other people in Chiota that although he was in the pay
of a white man, he had not in fact 'sold out'.

It is probable that Thomas's acceptance of David/*Kafudzi*'s divination and his
offer of tutelage was due, at least in part, to his growing sense of vocation and his
implicit ambition to become a high-level spirit-medium. If this was in fact the
case he made a good choice, for, as has already been shown, David/*Kafudzi* was a
medium who had extraordinary success and was in the process of becoming
widely known and respected. Thomas could only benefit from such respectable
credentials.

The final stage in Thomas's initiation involved a switch from David/*Kafudzi*
to Edward/*Chigara*. Apart from considerations relating to Tatenda village and the
reluctance of the villagers to accept David/*Kafudzi*'s pronouncements with respect to Thomas, it is quite likely that Thomas appreciated the added advantage
which would accrue to him, as a would-be high-level medium, from Edward/
Chigara's patronage. As with any other kind of professional training it is often

advantageous to possess more than one diploma, each with a different quality. By the time that Thomas had been through the final rite of *kudya muropa* and managed to restore his original good relations with David/*Kafudzi* he had the backing not only of the 'establishment' as represented by Edward/*Chigara*, but also the new wave as represented by the other.

Thomas's career as an independent spirit-medium began only when he moved, with his brother John, to the new village on the banks of the river, and once again he appears to have acquitted himself well. The fact that such stories as the one quoted about the rain had begun to circulate indicates that he was in fact beginning to build up his own reputation over and above the reputations of the mediums who had patronised him.

Even so, Thomas continued to work as a schoolmaster for he was not yet sufficiently well known to be able to devote himself full-time to mediumship. It is to the problem of this superficially strange combination of roles with their rather different belief systems to which I now turn.

The question of belief

Thomas was a schoolmaster who had been trained in Methodist and Roman Catholic colleges and yet he was a spirit-medium. John was a trained medical orderly and yet he had no doubts that his illness was an 'African' one. He refused treatment in hospital, even the taking of a lumbar puncture, and committed himself to the care of David/*Kafudzi*.

It is generally argued by educators and missionaries that 'irrational' beliefs in witchcraft, sorcery and spirit-mediumship must wither before the school text book and the pulpit, and yet in one of the areas of Rhodesia which has been most exposed to both of these forces such beliefs survive for the most part unquestioned.

The co-existence of two different belief systems is only surprising because of the initial assumption that they are mutually conflicting and contradictory. But, as Evans-Pritchard (1937) and later Gluckman (1955) have clearly demonstrated, this is a false assumption. Beliefs in ancestor spirits and witches do not preclude beliefs in atoms and germs; they complement them because they answer different questions of an existential nature. Epistemologically, there is no reason why both belief systems should not go hand in hand.

When John decided that his illness was 'African' and allowed himself to be treated almost exclusively by David/*Kafudzi* he did not deny 'Western' medicine. He merely regarded it as inappropriate in that particular instance. His belief in James' magic and Thomas's mediumship in no way contradicted his belief in the efficiency of the treatments that he himself gave as a medical orderly.

David/*Kafudzi* was himself no enemy of Western-style education or medicine. If he thought that patients would respond to treatment in hospital he did not hesitate to refer them either to the clinic in Mahusekwa Township or to Harare

105

Hospital in Salisbury. He merely insisted that hospital treatment could not be wholly effective by itself.

In most cases of sickness, patients are treated by both medium and doctor, and the two treatments are believed to be mutually necessary. The doctor's medicine is believed effective only if the patient is at one with the ancestors. Thus, although some symptoms are defined as indicating 'African' illness, the majority are treated under both systems, rather in the way in which Christians pray for their sick relatives.

Although the distinction between Zezuru and Western beliefs is largely a spurious one they are nevertheless kept discrete as the expressions 'African illness' (*chirwere che chivanhu*) and 'European illness' (*chirwere che cirungu*) imply. These belief systems not only explain unfortunate events, but also, in so doing, order, classify and make symbolic statements. A continuing belief in 'traditional' modes of explanation is therefore related to a continued commitment to 'traditional' social forms. Seen in this light, the discrete use of both 'Western' and 'African' belief systems is no stranger than the involvement of the people of Chiota in two kinds of social structure, the 'tribal' order of the Tribal Trust Land and the white dominated economic and governmental structure which encapsulates it.

In the next chapter where the whole question of the rise of spirit-mediums in the late 1950s will be raised, it will be argued that the rise of African nationalism with its new valuation of African-ness in Rhodesia led to a resurgence of commitment to 'traditional' beliefs and values. In this situation adherence to 'traditional' methods of curing was meaningful not only in the context of the internal relationships of the people of Chiota, but also with respect to overall black/white relationships in Southern Rhodesia. Thomas, and to a lesser extent John, participated in this cultural revival, and this may account at least in part for their attraction to David/*Kafudzi* and to their faith in Thomas's mediumship.

Thomas's trials and final installation as a spirit-medium had meaning, therefore, both in relation to Tatenda village politics, to the power politics of the high-level mediums of Chiota and to Thomas's personal vocational problems, and also in relation to the cultural revival which was linked to the genesis of African nationalist politics in Chiota.

6

Spirit-mediums and missionaries

This book has been concerned with the sociology of spirit-mediumship at various levels of social structure ranging from the role of low-level mediums in village politics through the internal power politics of high-level mediums to their role in the Shona Rebellion of 1896—7.

However, while the spirit-mediums of Chiota were engaged in the internal politics of the villages and the wider community, they were also involved in the conflict between black and white that dominated all Southern Rhodesia. Structurally opposed to Christianity and symbolic of African tradition, the spirit-mediums proliferated in Chiota Tribal Trust Land as a spontaneous religious reaction to a situation of head-on conflict between black and white nationalisms.

The development of African protest in Southern Rhodesia

Six years after the arrival of the British South Africa Company in Southern Rhodesia in 1890, first the Ndebele and then the Shona of central Mashonaland rose up in rebellion against the white settlers. Both the rebellions were inspired by religious leaders, in the case of the Ndebele by the Karanga Mwari cult and in the case of the Shona by certain of their spirit-mediums.

Ranger's account of the Shona Rebellion makes it clear that it was a response to a series of grave deprivations. The Shona had suffered from drought, an attack of rinderpest which had decimated their herds of cattle and also a plague of locusts which had attacked their crops. Furthermore they had lost their political autonomy to the British South Africa Company which had set up an administration and imposed a Hut Tax in 1893.

The rebellion was essentially a transformative movement,[1] in that it aimed to change radically the structure of Rhodesian society. The spirit-mediums, who articulated Shona protest, directed a sophisticated guerilla campaign which was supported by magic. With the blessing of the spirit-mediums they went into battle in the firm belief that the bullets of the enemy would turn to water and that the hooves of the colonists horses would be burned as they crossed 'doctored' rivers.

Not only were outlying farmsteads attacked, but also the mission stations and it was in that sense a holy war. This was also the view of the settlers, for the missionaries believed that when the rebellion was finally put down the spirit-

107

mediums would be discredited and with them faith in 'traditional' religion. The way to Christianity would be open.

The rebellion was put down in 1897, after which resistance to the whites continued sporadically until 1900 in areas of Mashonaland which had not involved themselves in the main rebellion.[2] Otherwise the general trend was that the Shona and Ndebele, who previously had adamantly rejected the presence of the whites and participation in their culture, now gave themselves over to accepting the new *status quo* and participating in it. As the whites had hoped, with the failure of the rebellion, 'there *was* a great missionary break-through in Southern Rhodesia . . . though it was probably based on more material foundations than missionary realisation of Shona religious sense' (Ranger 1967 : 337). 'The missions now entered upon a period of great power and influence during which they were, as sour Native administrators remarked, the real rulers of large areas of rural Mashonaland.' (Ranger 1967 : 338)

Ranger notes that the failure of the rebellion was crippling for the Shona, who lost most of their leaders, and he adds that 'for some twenty years after the risings the Shona made no significant move into new kinds of opposition'. It would seem that during this time, mission activity went well ahead. The Shona tacitly accepted the 'premise of inequality' imposed by the white colonisers, and the demand for education grew as they set about learning new skills for a new situation.

The first signs of protest occurred in 1920, with the formation of the Southern Rhodesian Bantu Voter's Association. It was a reformist movement[3] for it merely sought legitimate changes without actually challenging the system. The following extract from the aims and objects of the association (quoted in Shamuyarira 1965 : 30, 31) speaks for itself:

We believe that justice must be done to our people and their legitimate rights respected; we believe that only by means of industrial education, a test of Christianity, our people will rise gradually in the scale of civilisation and that religion must be fostered to grow as the true foundation of a man's character.

Work shall be effected by constitutional resolutions and peaceful propaganda, and by consulting the Native Affairs Department, MPs and missionaries.[4]

Shamuyarira (1965 : 31) writes: 'It was in fact a mild constitution, written by an obedient group of educated men.' The same point is made by Richard Gray (Gray 1960 : 316) of a similar reformist movement, the Bantu Congress of Southern Rhodesia, which was also elitist and restricted in both aims and methods.

During and after the Second World War different types of movements arose, but they were originally urban-based, concerned with the conditions of urban employment and dwelling. They were slightly more radical than previous movements, beginning to challenge what they called 'Southern Rhodesia's Undemocratic Native Policy' (Gray 1960 : 323) and were a response to specific deprivations. Africans in town began to be aware of their poor conditions both in contrast to the whites, and also as compared with affairs before the Urban Areas Act.[5] In addition, many Africans had participated not as Africans but as soldiers in the war, which had led to a greater questioning of the racial segregation and discrimination they found in Rhodesian society on their return.

In 1957 the first truly nationalist party was formed, the African National Congress, which included both rural and urban Africans from all over Rhodesia. It was banned by the government in 1957, and was followed in January 1960 by the National Democratic Party (NDP), which was in turn banned in December 1962. It was succeeded by the Zimbabwe African People's Union (ZAPU) within ten days.

ZAPU met the fate of its predecessors: it was to be succeeded by two rival parties, the People's Caretaker Council (PCC), under the leadership of Joshua Nkomo, who had previously led ZAPU, and the Zimbabwe African National Union (ZANU), led by the Rev. Sithole, who had broken away from Nkomo's leadership.

The split in the nationalist movement resulted in a state of virtual civil war in the African townships as rival factions fought one another. Each party attempted to eliminate the other until in August 1964 they were both banned and a 'State of Emergency' declared (*Central African Examiner*, September 1964).

The Rhodesian Government was meanwhile attempting to acquire independence from Britain on its own terms. The Prime Minister, Mr Ian Smith, held a meeting of African chiefs at Domboshawa in October 1964 (the Domboshawa Indaba) and they unanimously declared their support for him. The British government, however, queried the representative status of the chiefs and declined to grant Smith's government independence.[6] Finally Rhodesia declared itself independent unilaterally on 11 November 1965. Since then, in spite of action on the part of the United Nations and Britain, including a 'sanctions war', the Smith government has remained secure. By 1966 it appeared to both the Africans of Rhodesia, and the whites of Rhodesia, that African nationalism had been crushed and that the whites had at least won the first major round of the struggle.

The government responded to nationalist parties with every weapon at its disposal, erecting a formidable body of legislation based on the Law and Order (Maintenance) Act of 1957. By means of this legislation it was possible not only to ban parties, newspapers (the *Daily News* in August 1964) but also to detain and restrict persons without trial. The legislation was efficiently backed by a large police force aided by an informer network of some size, so that overt nationalist politics were effectively silenced in Rhodesia. Meetings of over three persons were banned so that any form of political activity without prior permission from the police was circumscribed.

The uneasy calm of post-UDI Rhodesia rested basically on the superior force of the white government and should not be interpreted to mean that the African population had abandoned its nationalistic ideals. If anything nationalist sentiment became stronger, in reaction to the increasingly repressive nature of

109

white domination. Overt expression of such sentiments was slight and was restricted to the support given to terrorist incursions in certain farming areas.[7] In 1972 the Pearce Commission surprised itself and the Rhodesian government in finding that an overwhelming majority of the African population continues steadfast in its opposition to white domination.[8]

The religious side of nationalist politics

The rise of the African nationalist movement in Rhodesia was accompanied by an upsurge of cultural nationalism. Not only were white political institutions under attack, but also many of the premises of their culture. Particularly significant was the new emphasis on 'traditional institutions', especially spirit-mediumship. The political struggle became a religious one as many Africans returned to their 'traditional' religious rituals at the expense of the Christian churches.

Ranger (1967 : 382) notes that the nationalist leaders 'discovered that their own critical and selective attitude towards the life of the West was very different from the emulative acceptance of the early association . . .'

Nathan Shamuyarira puts the general case succinctly:

The NDP was concerned to find a spiritual and cultural base for African Nationalism. The party encouraged its supporters to value those things which were African customs, names, music, dress, religion and food and much else . . . In religion young Africans increasingly rejected the view encouraged among their elders by missionaries that worshipping ancestral spirits or gods of idols was heathen superstition . . . Africans feel they can worship most effectively through the intermediary of ancestors they know. I heard one girl in the Mhondore reserve tell her mother: 'God is for us all, but this Jesus is for the Europeans and the Jews.' Another angry young man retorted: 'In actual fact Jesus is like a big Colonial Secretary for the Missionaries. They use his preachings to blind us, while Europeans take our land and heritage.' (1965 : 62).

In rural areas meetings became political gatherings and more — social occasions where old friendships were renewed and new ones made, past heritage was revived through prayers and traditional singing with African instruments, ancestral spirits were evoked to guide and lead the new nation. Christianity and civilisation took a back seat, and new forms of worship, and new attitudes were thrust forward dramatically. Although all attendants wore western clothes (sometimes accompanied by African-made fur hats and sandal shoes) and cars and loudspeakers were seen everywhere as signs of the scientific age, the spirit pervading the meetings was African and the desire was to put the twentieth century in an African context. (1965 : 68, 69).

Shamuyarira (1965 : 146) saw that Christianity was being rejected and criticised because it remained 'in political terms, the white man's church. Africans tended to see the church, the government, the Native Affairs department, education, industrialisation — all the ills and all the benefits of the white man — as

110

inextricably interlaced' and because it was unable to provide a 'spiritual and moral base' for African nationalism.

Both Ranger and Shamuyrarira affirm that the leaders of the nationalist parties encouraged a return to the 'traditional' religions of the Ndebele and Shona, and they give examples of how this actually happened at political meetings. Ranger (1967 : 383) notes specifically the involvement of mediums in Chiweshe and in the Darwin area and how 'one of the results of this new sense on the part of African politicians of the importance of the rural masses was a revival of the *political influence* [my italics] of the Mwari priests [of the Ndebele and Karanga] and the spirit mediums. Nationalist leaders discovered that they still possessed influence and courted them; the religious leaders regained some of the confidence lost in the 1920s and 1930s.'

In the *Central African Examiner* of December 1963, a Mr T. Chaita launched an attack on the churches in Rhodesia for having condemned the indigenous Shona religion that they found. This was succeeded by some interesting replies. In the March issue, R.L. Marahwa wrote that Africans quickly gave way to Christianity and forgot the efficacy of the prayers they had one time addressed to their spirits. However, doubts had begun to arise as to the efficacy of the new religion. He then noted that as politics entered the arena, Christianity was opposed for being a peaceful way of perpetuating colonialism . . . Africans lost faith in the religion they could not fully understand. 'They now look back with admiration to their old ways which Christianity forced them to forget.'

Mr Maronda wrote in the April issue: 'It is unfortunate that the gospellers . . . came to Zimbabwe . . . carrying five different things on, in or with them. These were: a white skin, a Bible in the right hand coat pocket, a sharp sweet tongue, some gunpowder in the left trouser pocket, and IGNORANCE of the Black African's philosophy of life.'

Having observed the many iniquities of Christianity in Rhodesia, not least that it 'exploited him (the Black man) causing fatal blows to a once flourishing culture', he ended by exhorting the Africans of Rhodesia to go forward with a 'renaissance of the Black African's religion'.

A popular nationalist political song gives an idea of the importance of this new cultural nationalism.

Munhumutapa, mambo wedu	Munhumutapa is our Lord
Munyika ino ye Zimbabwe.	In this land of Zimbabwe.
Lobengula, mambo wedu.	Lobengula is our sovereign.
Uripi Munhumutapa?	But where are you, Munhumutapa?
Zimbabwe, nyika yomutema;	Zimbabwe is the land of the black man;
Zimbabwe, zinyika redu.	Zimbabwe our great country.
Chitungwisa, makatora	You (whites) took Chitungwisa
(Gomba risina mwana)	(An adulterer has no child)
Kugara muri moga.	To live on your own.
Batsirai vana venyu,	Help your children,

Vanhu vose vanofira,	All people are dying,
Nyika yedu ye Zimbabwe,	This land of Zimbabwe,
Rizere mukaka neuchi,	Flowing with milk and honey,
Nyika yomushu mutema.	Is the land of the black man.
Zvirwere, nzara nenyota;	Sickness, hunger and thirst;
Minda yese makatora.	You have taken all the fields.
Rufu rwako Chaminuka,	It is your death, Chaminuka,
Uripi, Munhumutapa?	Where are you, Munhumutapa?
Unoda kugara nesu,	You want to live with us,
Ngavakauye tivatonge.	So let them come and we shall rule them.
Tichaudza vanhu vose	We shall respect everyone
NeupfumihweZimbabwe.	With the wealth of Zimbabwe.

In this song, which uses a certain amount of biblical imagery, Zimbabwe is portrayed as a rich and fertile land, which has been raped by the white man. Zimbabwe, a woman, is married to the black man. All that she produces, therefore, is rightfully the black man's, even though she is living in adultery with the white man. The men who are begged to help are the true 'husbands', the great heroes of the past. Lobengula the king of the Amandebele, Chaminuka and Munhumutapa. The past is called upon to solve the problems of the present.

It is important to note that the cultural and religious aspects of African nationalism had their counterpart in white nationalism. The claims of the whites to the right to rule the country were justified by the belief that they were defending 'Western Christian civilised standards' against 'communism' and the 'Black peril'. Not only did they give marked emphasis to Christianity, but also to their own culture heroes, especially Cecil John Rhodes whose tomb in the Matopos Hills became a centre for pilgrimage and the focus for annual rituals to commemorate his death. It is ironic that he died a confirmed atheist.

The situation in Chiota

The general political and religious trends which have been outlined for Rhodesia as a whole, apply especially to Chiota. Its people were involved in the rebellion of 1896, having been exposed very early to both the white administration and Christianity, the mission of Waddilove (then Nenguo Mission) being established in 1892. Before the rebellion the mission had made little headway; chief Nenguo merely made land available but did not become a Christian himself. Even after the rebellion, there was no sudden turn to the churches, and it seems as though the great breakthrough occurred in the 1930s when there was increased demand for education which was provided by the missions.

Nathan Shamuyarira supports the view that Chiota people opted for education, Christianity and the acquisition of the new skills and artifacts with enthusiasm. The prestige that had accrued to the mediums and the old leaders passed largely to the new educated elite. 'By far the strongest driving force to gain education', he says, 'is that Africans see in it the power to do what the European has been able to do . . . ' (1965 : 116).

There are Anglican, Roman Catholic and Methodist schools and churches in Chiota, but the last of these three has had the most profound influence. The Nenguo Circuit in the District of Marandellas had the greatest number of churches and schools. The Circuit was organised under an African minister who lived in Chiota and each church had its own evangelist and church committees. Members of the Methodist Church were expected to pay 2s 6d per month in 'class money' which was then sent to District headquarters, which then decided what money should be spent on the Circuit. The Circuit also encouraged women's and men's bible study groups and the women's club (Ruwadzano) was very popular as a forum for women's affairs. Each church had its own group of women who dressed up in black skirts, white blouses and red jackets to attend their weekly meetings.[9]

The Methodist Church, like the others, was especially involved in education and by the side of each church or chapel there appeared a school. In the 1930s and 1940s school buildings were financed by the local communities but the teachers were paid by the missions. However, latterly, government has assumed this responsibility and only buildings and materials and additional teachers are paid for by the communities represented through school committees. There were only six schools in Chiota that went up as far as standard VI in 1965 and there were widespread protests that the schools should all complete the primary cycle and that a secondary school should be established in the area. The wave of cultural nationalism in Chiota did nothing to dampen the almost universal craving for education.

The Methodist Church, more than the others, has always been strongly opposed to any manifestation of African traditional religion and in the days when they controlled the schools completely it is said that they expelled the children of any adult who had been involved in traditional ritual. But perhaps their most powerful sanction was applied through women church members. The Methodists forbade their members to take alcoholic beverages, which meant that women converts could no longer brew beer. Not only did this have a rather dampening effect on the daily round, but it also meant that rituals which depended on beer (*mapira*) could not always be held.

During the thirties, forties and fifties, then, Christianity and education made great strides and the prestige that had in the past been accorded to the old wise men and the spirit-mediums was transferred to the new men, the evangelists, teachers and businessmen who were Christian and who could read and write not only in the vernacular but also in English. It seems to have been widely believed by the Africans of Chiota that Christian education was the way to equality with the whites and to bringing about the brotherhood of man that the churches preached.

But all this was at the level of public social behaviour on the wider stage that had been set with the inclusion of Chiota in a wider society. The beliefs themselves did not die out, nor did they cease to be used; they went underground and the open collective rituals associated with spirit-mediumship gave way to more secretly held consultations with the herbalist/diviners (*nganga*). Although the white missionaries may have thought that their converts had been totally weaned from their original beliefs, this had not in fact occurred. Indeed even after the rise of spirit-mediumship in the late fifties I was able to observe that some Methodist evangelists continued to keep a foot in both camps. They attended church in public and worshipped the ancestors indirectly by contributing in cash or kind to the cost of rituals.

But the situation of overt Christianity with traditional religious forms more or less kept underground was to change dramatically in the early 1960s.

The first four months of my fieldwork in Chiota coincided with the last four months of ZANU and PCC (see above, p. 109). Political activity mainly took the form of acts of aggression against churches, churchmen and those concerned with the dipping of cattle. In addition there were occasional incidents when persons were beaten up for supposedly belonging to ZANU (Chiota was solidly PCC). Churches were burned at Chakadiyi (Methodist in Nenguo chieftaincy), St James (Anglican, Nenguo chieftaincy) and St Peters (Anglican, Chiota chieftaincy), while St Annas (Roman Catholic, Nenguo) had its windows stoned out. Two evangelists at Rupere Methodist church in the Nenguo chieftaincy had their houses burned down, and six persons led by the chairman of the PCC in Chiota were sentenced to prison for this crime. In August 1964 a number of people had their houses burned, notably the African cattle dipping supervisor (a government official). Dip-tanks were also attacked, and there was a move to force people to surrender their cattle dipping cards to the nationalist youth for burning.[10] The *Weekend Daily News* of 15 August commented on these events: 'A tense atmosphere of terror and fear reigns in the hitherto quiet Chiota reserve, Marandellas, where acts of violence and arson have been carried out since the beginning of this month.'

Subsequent to the banning of PCC and ZANU, no more violence or arson took place and people were loathe to express their political views publicly for fear of arrest and restriction or detention. Even the singing of political songs, which had been a feature of most gatherings and beer drinks, came to an end. Hopes that the British government would effect a solution in Rhodesia rose and fell. so that by November 1966, when I left Chiota, almost all hope for success had disappeared.

On the religious front the violence practised against church buildings and against certain churchmen was accompanied by a dropping-off in church attendance and a marked increase in the number of ancestral rituals performed, especially those to initiate new spirit-mediums. The two phenomena did not go without notice or comment in Chiota.

Many informants asserted that there had been a tremendous revival of the

114

'traditional' religion in Chiota. They pointed to the ever increasing number of mediums and one woman complained that if it went on much longer like this there would be no-one left in the reserve who was not a spirit-medium. They pointed also to the increased status and prestige of mediumship, and stressed that it was significantly the young men who were most prominent in the movement, people who had hitherto scorned what they considered to be out-of-date customs, only held by the old people.

There were many instances of people who had been active church members foregoing their Christian affiliation to become spirit-mediums. One woman had been a medium before joining the church in the late 1940s. She had burnt the spirit's ritual paraphernalia. However, in 1965 she became ill, went to divine and found that the sickness was being caused by the spirit that had possessed her and which was expressing its anger that its host had abandoned it for the church. She was told to re-equip herself with her paraphernalia and to brew a *bira*. She thus left the church and became a medium once more.

The experiences of David Mudiwa have already been told (see above, pp. 38–42). In a way, his transformation from Methodist preacher to high-level spirit-medium was the most dramatic instance of the widespread disillusionment with the Christian churches and the chapel in which he had preached and which nestled in the shadow of his large seance house, a guest house for visitors, was a constant reminder of what had happened.

The Methodist reaction

The *Rhodesia Herald* contained the following report in its issue of 30 December 1964: ' "Our African Christians are very brave", said the superintendent of the Methodist Church (British) in Rhodesia, the Rev. J.H. Lawrence. "But, as they say, they have a grass roof over their heads". There had been threats of beatings and hut burnings in the Marandellas area, and church attendance had been markedly affected, he said.'

The Methodists as a whole were inclined to interpret their sudden loss of congregations in terms of political 'intimidators'. The Methodist minister in Chiota who retired in January 1965 said that Christianity was dead in the area because of intimidation and his successor told of how he had been visited by a spirit-medium who had come to confront him and had then sent his followers around in the villages entreating the villagers to leave the church and return to their spirit-mediums.

At the quarterly meeting of the Nenguo Circuit held in April 1965, the Methodists had to face the serious financial consequences of the dropping off of membership. It was agreed that the causes of the exodus from the churches were intimidation and the class money, which, at 2s 6d a month, they thought rather high.

One preacher, however, stood up and while agreeing that the class money and

115

intimidation might be the immediate and surface causes of their problems, said the matter really went deeper than that. It was no use trying to rid a field of thorn trees just by cutting their branches, he said, you had to get at the roots. He expressed the view that the fall-off in church attendance had deeper causes than those which had been singled out.

And he was right. Even though one might interpret the cause of the drop in church attendance as 'intimidation', this could not explain either the fact that those who no longer attended church were disillusioned with Christianity (they did not hold secret meetings) and even less the spontaneous rate of increase in spirit-mediumship throughout Chiota. Those who attribute large-scale protest to 'intimidation' usually have very good reasons for doing so, for it is one way of denying large-scale dissatisfaction.

Zezuru heroes and Christian saints

The explanations that the people of Chiota gave for the decline in church attendance and the increase in the number of spirit-mediums and their enhanced prestige varied, yet they all correlated the two facts and related them to black/white relations in Rhodesia.

The basic religious explanation related to the problem of understanding why African nationalism in Rhodesia had not had the success that it had had in Zambia and Malawi and in other African countries further afield. It was felt that the movement had so far failed to bring about results because it did not have the essential protection of the ancestors who had abandoned their people as punishment for having been so long neglected. The myth of the tree without a name (*muti usina zita*) states the position.

Long ago, before the coming of the whites, there was a tree somewhere near the present Waddilove Mission. Passing travellers used to stop there and pray to the ancestors whereupon food in the form of stiff porridge (*sadza*) and meat would fall from the branches. When the white men arrived they were astonished and asked a local African for the secret behind the tree. He (the primordial sell-out) told all and the white men were able, with their superior technology, to destroy the tree's miraculous powers. When the white men no longer rule in Rhodesia the tree will once more provide food for the hungry traveller.

Not only was it necessary to return to the ancestors in order to acquire their vital protection once more, it was also necessary to leave the Christian churches in order to escape from the control which the whites were believed to exercise through them. Jesus Christ was seen as a white hero spirit who was directing white political action in the way in which Zezuru hero spirits do for their descendants. Ironically the very parallel between the Christian saints and Shona heroes and ancestors which the missionaries had first made in order to explain Christian doctrine was now being used to reject it. This conception of Christianity and 'traditional' Zezuru religion as being much the same kinds of faith, but

116

manipulated by different groups of people was justified by empirical observations of white ancestor-worship. That flowers were put regularly on graves, that there should be annual rites at Cecil Rhodes' tomb and that the local farmers should meet regularly at weekends to drink beer and roast meet[11] was ample evidence that the ancestors and the heroes of the whites were fundamental to Christianity.

A number of people in Chiota went beyond these explanations and felt that Christianity had played a more direct part in the maintenance of white domination. They suggested that the idea of the brotherhood of man was what they preached but not what they practised; that the class money was used to build large churches in Salisbury before building schools in the African areas and that the ideology of the white government was based on Christianity. African nationalist leaders in the area went even further than this and stated that 'traditional' culture had to be encouraged as an essential element in the nationalist movement. The spirit-mediums could provide the symbols of coherence which were so important.

Here then is a further example of the way in which explanation in terms of religious beliefs reflects the social context. The explanation for the failure of the African nationalist movement in terms of the withdrawal of ancestral protection and the myth of the tree with no name say much the same thing as the other more 'empirical' explanations in that they attribute to Christianity a positive role in the maintenance of white dominance and offer a return to the ancestors — to 'traditional' values — as a solution.

We can now examine some of the sociological factors which may account, at least in part, for the choice of spirit-mediumship as a focus for cultural nationalist aspirations.

The African past

The colonial history of Rhodesia is short, and the past is regarded by the Africans as a paradise which was corrupted by colonisation. At that time Africans controlled their own destiny.

Through the institution of spirit-mediumship the heroes of the past actually converse with the living, and in the dramatic context of *bira* rituals time is momentarily abolished in the meeting of past and present. Another nationalist song illustrates the way in which history was telescoped:

Ridza ngoma Chaminuka!	Play your drum, Chaminuka!
Yava nguva yako	How your time has come
Yokufudza muZimbabwe.	To herd in Zimbabwe.
Ridza ngoma Chaminuka.	Play your drum, Chaminuka.
Tinosangana mukufa	We shall meet in death
Neropa raMwari (Pari)	Through the blood of God (Pari)
Rakaparadzirwa nyika,	Which was shed for the country,
Tinosanganiswa.	We shall be brought together.

117

Spirits of protest

Kwaivepo baba wedu	There he was, our father,
Waigara Chitungwiza	There at Chitungwiza,
Zita ravo, Chaminuka,	His name was Chaminuka,
Mufemberi wedu.	And he was our prophet.
Vakatongwa neMabunhu,	He was judged by the Boers,
Vakaenda navo	He went away with them
Kumusha wavo, England	To their home, England
Vakavauraya.	And there they killed him.
Vakatuma vakomana	They sent their youths
Muti vavabaye,	To kill him,
Nokuti vanotevera Nkomo	Because he was a follower of Nkomo
Vakavauraya.	They murdered him.

In this song Chaminuka, whose medium was a popular Shona leader in the nineteenth century when they were fighting the Ndebele is portrayed as a follower of Joshua Nkomo, the leader of the present-day struggle with the whites. The rivalry between the Ndebele and the Shona is concealed by attributing Chaminuka's death to the Boers[12] and interesting use is made of the similarity between the two words 'Mwari' (God) and 'Pari' (Dr Parirenyatwa)' 'Pari' was an African Nationalist leader who died mysteriously (some believe murdered) on a level-crossing on the road between Salisbury and Bulawayo. The song emphasises the co-operation between the dead and the living in the struggle for independence.

Whilst the spirit-mediums bring the heroes of the past into contact with the living, the rituals that surround them are truly African occasions.

Ritual, music and dancing

Apart from language, the most distinctive features of Zezuru culture[13] in relation to that of the whites are etiquette, music and dancing, all of which flourish in the ritual context.[14]

Music is provided by thumb-pianos (*mbira*) and rattles (*magosho*) and sometimes drums (*ngoma*). The thumb-piano is essential to spirit seances and the keen musician is capable of playing the right tunes to bring out the spirits, and to set the rhythm for dancing.

Nearly all the *mbira* players in Chiota were young men who had learnt to play quite recently. The one old *mbira* player whom I met claimed that until 1960 he had been the only player for miles around and that he was able to cope with whatever rituals took place. Nowadays, he observed, many young boys were learning to play and they were all in constant demand at rituals. The *mbira* was so popular that it was actually challenging the popularity of the guitar among the young.

But the *mbira* have to be produced as do other artifacts such as ritual swordsticks, knobkerries, axes, spears and head-dresses of fur or black ostrich feathers.

118

Old skills have been revived and those who are able to make these objects have their order-books full.

Ritual, then, carried with it an aura of cultural commitment. But while it valorised African culture, it also excluded certain symbols of European culture. Shoes could not be worn at rituals; women, who had their hair straightened or were wearing earrings and make-up, were frequently turned away and wrist watches had to be removed before entering the seance houses.

But there are other sociological reasons why the cultural aspects of African Nationalism should be focused on the spirit-mediums and not, for example, on the chiefs, who also might also be classed as 'traditional' figures.

Mediums and chiefs

According to Government ideology the chiefs in Rhodesia are the leaders of their people, the 'fathers' of their 'children'. However, as has already been argued earlier in this book (see above, p. 9) the chiefs not only represent their people to the government but the government to the people; they are government servants as well as tribal leaders.

Chiefs who displease the government are removed from office and chiefs who displease their people are ignored by them. In the present situation in Rhodesia where the government is in conflict with the African people, the chiefs are forced into an almost intolerable position.[15] In Chiota the chiefs managed their position by trying to please both sides. At the 'Domboshawa Indaba' (see above, p. 109) they voted in favour of independence under a white minority government but when they returned to their people they said that that was not what they *really* wanted. Rumours actually circulated to the effect that the Chiota chiefs had voted against the government, which could not have been true as the vote was unanimously in favour.

Chiefs, then, derive their authority, in the last analysis from government support; the clear signs of this in Chiota are the circles of white stones which the government installed near chiefs' houses as landing grounds for helicopters. Their authority over their people is based on the powers of coercion that the government controls. If they were to become involved with African nationalist politics they would no longer be chiefs.[16]

The spirit-mediums, on the other hand, control no physical sanctions to enforce their decisions, and the threats that they may make in trance are only effective if those who are threatened choose to believe in them. The authority of spirit-mediums depends therefore not on coercion but on consensus. In the political sphere the chiefs lie half-way between the Africans and the whites; in the religious sphere the spirit-mediums stand structurally opposed to Christianity.

Of the five chiefs in Chiota, three at least maintained close relations of dependence with the most popular spirit-mediums in their area. One chief provided his car and himself as driver for the spirit-medium that he consulted and another firmly believed that he owed his survival as a chief to a high-level medium. Chiefs are issued with pistols by government for self-defence. One of the sons of this particular chief had used the gun in an argument and seriously wounded his antagonist. The case was taken to the police and it seemed certain that one of the consequences would be the deposition of the chief. The chief, however, consulted a spirit-medium who promised him that all would be well and indeed the case was dropped.

The chiefs need the mediums as they need a certain measure of popularity. Their deference to the spirit-mediums is a statement of their respect for common consensus which the mediums enshrine.[17]

Spirit-mediums, then are effective as a focus for nationalist sentiment because they bring the past to the present, because their ritual encourages essentially traditional activities, but above all because they are the people whose very authority is given by public opinion and who are unequivocally opposed structurally to Christianity.

Hope and despair

Prior to the banning of the African Nationalist parties in 1964 and Mr Smith's declaration of independence from Britain in 1965 the Africans of Chiota were confident that majority rule would soon be established in Rhodesia. The spontaneous emergence of new spirit-mediums in Chiota was a popular manifestation of this confidence. However, after the events of 1964 and 1965 hope turned almost to despair as it became clear that majority rule would not easily be achieved. The nationalist movement had split down the middle, Africans had killed Africans, Mr Smith's government had shown its strength and the British government had failed to do anything much about it.

Although there was a widespread feeling that Mr Smith's success was largely due to the British government's complaisance, there was also a certain amount of self-recrimination. The feeling grew that the breakdown of solidarity in the nationalist movement had been the crucial factor in its downfall; as the government's repressive measures became more and more severe, the effectiveness was seen to be largely due to the active help of numerous black police and informers. Just as the whites of Rhodesia see any deviation from their racialist and segregationist line as due to 'communists' and 'subversives', so the Africans began their hunt for 'sell-outs', those who had taken sides with the whites. The confrontation between white and black had been diverted into a search for the enemy within, in an attempt to re-establish solidarity.[18] Although there is little doubt that the dissensions within the ranks of African nationalism were a reaction to the repressive measures of the government and the frustration that these entailed, and although such dissension was propitious for and therefore encouraged by the government, the people of Chiota realised that their failure to maintain a solid front had been a decisive factor in Mr Smith's victory.

The search for 'informers' and 'sell-outs' was accompanied in the religious sphere by a new preoccupation with witches and sorcerers, or, rather, a new preoccupation with the public accusations of them. The most popular spirit-mediums in Chiota were those who were believed capable of detecting witchcraft and sorcery and for exorcising the former.

David/*Kafudzi* was perhaps the best-known detector of witchcraft and sorcery and clients sometimes chose to go to him for divination for this reason. He stressed the danger of medicines (*miti*) and demanded that those who had used them for whatever purpose should bring them to him to be destroyed. At weekends he brought out the pile that had accumulated over the previous week and burned them.[19] Many women were accused of being possessed by witching spirits (*shave ro uroyi*). Exorcism involved first of all bringing the woman into trance by her witching spirit so that she might confess. After this the woman, in trance, was beaten by the medium using a thorn branch and then sent into the bush. The spirit was believed to leave her and to enter into an animal such as a hare (*tsuro*).[20] Accusations of witchcraft were sometimes traumatic for the supposed witch, but she soon found that she was in the company of many more, for the seance house often contained ten or more undergoing treatment.[21] Accused witches learned to accept their unfortunate condition and co-operated fully in order to be exorcised. David/*Kafudzi* often began his seances by asking whether the witches were present. They held up their hands and told in turn the dreams that they had had the previous night.

The accent on witchcraft that characterised much of the divination at David/*Kafudzi*'s seance house was also a feature of his disciples, the mediums whom he himself initiated. One such, who again was also a teacher, gave a speech at the opening of his own new seance house. The speech was an allegory of the political situation in Rhodesia. He said that in the olden days when two villages were in conflict, the village which had the greater internal unity would vanquish the other. Witchcraft, he said, was a source of disunity and he would dedicate his work as a spirit-medium to its eradication in Chiota.

It seems that the battle with witchcraft was an attempt to control a situation which had got out of control; the conflict between white and black had been transmuted into a conflict between the ancestors and witchcraft. 'The atmosphere of myth and magic frightens me . . . ' writes Fanon (1967 : 43) from the Algerian perspective.

By terrifying me, it integrates me in the traditions and the history of my district or of my tribe, and at the same time it reassures me, it gives me a status, as it were, an identification paper . . . Believe me, the Zombies are more terrifying than the settlers; and in consequence the problem is no longer that of keeping oneself right with the colonial world and its barbed-wire entanglements, but of considering three times before urinating, spitting or going out into the night.

The supernatural, magical powers reveal themselves as essentially personal; the settler's powers are infinitely shrunken, stamped with their alien origin. We no longer really need to fight against them since what counts is the frightening enemy created by myths. We perceive that all is settled by a paramount confrontation on the phantasmic plane.

It seemed that in Chiota the spirit-mediums who had once heralded the triumphant return of the ancestors and the realisation of nationalist ambitions were now the arbiters of despondancy and despair. Now that political activity had been effectively repressed religion remained as an outlet for the pent up hostilities generated by the colonial situation.

Conclusions

In 1896–7 spirit-mediums articulated common grievances in central Mashonaland and were able to co-ordinate them into a rebellion whose aim was to sweep the colonists from their country.

Seventy years later, in the same area of Southern Rhodesia, the spirit-mediums, after a long period of relative inactivity, once more became important in a situation where white dominance was again under challenge. At first, with the stirrings of African nationalism, they became the focusing points of African cultural nationalism. The mushrooming of spirit-mediums over Chiota Tribal Trust Land and other areas nearby and the decline of church congregations was a dramatic affirmation of a new faith in old ways and a rejection of European cultural domination. Later, when overt political activities were repressed the spirit-mediums continued to flourish and to hold their rituals but the emphasis that accompanied the widespread despair of the people shifted to a preoccupation with witchcraft and sorcery.

Although there is evidence to show that the religious restoration which took place in Chiota was also taking place in other Tribal Trust Lands of central Mashonaland,[22] the religious reaction to the political situation was negligable amongst the Korekore[23] and amongst the Budya[24] and the Karanga it took the form of a proliferation of Zionist cult groups similar to those described in the case of South Africa by Sundkler (1961), and although I am not able to suggest reasons for this differential reaction in other areas of Southern Rhodesia, I have tried to reveal the logic of the situation in Chiota.

Chiota people as a whole were supporters of African nationalist ideals, and much of social life was taken up with problems which were either directly or indirectly a result of the conflict between white and black in Southern Rhodesia. Spirit-mediumship was a ready made institution which could be called upon to give meaning to the restored faith in African tradition and custom. Furthermore, the spirit-mediums are recognised as such for their ability to satisfy their followers. They assumed the role as symbols of African-ness against European-ness;

Spirit-mediums and missionaries

they were opposed to the missionaries as the heroes of the Shona past were opposed to Jesus Christ.

Notes

Introduction

1 The Chiota African council is made up five chiefs, four ward headmen and fifteen elected councillors (see p. 6). The elected members of the council tended to take a more objective stance with respect to their relations with the government than did the chiefs and headmen.

2 Gelfand, writing in 1959, thought that the prospects for the survival of Zezuru religion were small. 'For each year that passes by less and less of the ritual is being carried out . . . The most significant fact is that the educated man is hardly ever seen at one of the Mashona religious ceremonies. Practically every African who attends is one who, while he may have been to a village school or mission, can hardly speak English'. (Gelfand 1959 : 12). In Chiota it was rare not to find educated people attending rituals and when they didn't they often participated indirectly by helping with the expenses.

1. The secular background

1 The word 'tradition' is here put in inverted commas to emphasise the fact that it is essentially a folk concept, which refers to a static tribal pre-colonial past. As an analytical concept 'tradition' can be very misleading for there is no reason to suppose that social change in Rhodesia began with colonisation.

2 See chapter 4 for a discussion of certain differences of religious organisation and social structure between the Zezuru and the Korekore.

3 For an excellent analysis of the effects of the Land Husbandry Act see Garbett (1963b).

4 For an analysis of the structural position of Rhodesia chiefs see Holleman's study *Chief, Council and Commissioner* (1969).

5 A few Zezuru do work on European-owned farms, but the majority of such farm workers are immigrants from Malawi. Amongst the people of Chiota there is a certain disdain for this kind of work.

6 Women form the stable element of the population of Chiota and are thus many times more *au fait* with village political affairs than their husbands. At a rain-making ritual in 1965 the head of the royal lineage of a tribal ward was invoking his patrilineal ancestors. After the third generation there was an embarrassed pause until his wife, who was seated just behind him, was able to prompt him in audible whispers for the most distant generations.

2. Magico-religious beliefs

1 For an analysis of this question see chapter 6.

2   *Shave* spirits, similar both structurally and in their function to those of the
     Zezuru, feature in much of the ethnography of Central Africa, while the
     syndrome of outsider/amoral/individual shown by these spirits as against
     inside/moral/communal shown by ancestor spirits seems to be much more
     widespread. The same opposition is clear from Beattie's Nyoro material,
     with the *mizimu* (ancestor spirits) and the white *mbandwa* (spirit, power)
     who are moral and associated with social groupings as against the black
     mbandwa, who are 'immigrants' in Bunyoro, amoral and highly individual-
     istic (Beattie 1961, 1964). A similar situation exists in Kalabari, for whom
     Horton has distinguished three categories of 'free spirits'. The ancestor
     spirits (*duen*) are associated with lineages and concerned with the lineage
     moral order; the village heroes (*am'oru*) uphold the moral order of villages
     (although they are believed to have come from outside, they are neverthe-
     less linked to social groupings); and the water people (*owuamapu*) who are
     not associated with social groupings, are external, associated with natural
     phenomena and with 'human behaviour which deviates either above or
     below social norms' (Horton 1961 : 201). Horton is then able to add the
     further opposition of 'nature/culture', noting that 'both nature and deviant
     activities are in a sense external to the established social order maintained
     by heroes and ancestors' (Horton 1962 : 202).

3   The term for both witch and sorcerer is *muroyi*, but distinctions are made
     descriptively depending on the context. Gelfand reports having found the
     term '*muroyi we masikati*' (*muroyi* of mid-day) to refer to sorcerers, which,
     he claims are generally male. (Gelfand 1964b : 34). In another context he
     notes: 'Male witches are much rarer than female witches and their practice
     of witchcraft is different. Instead of moving around at night in the com-
     pany of other witches and eating the flesh of the dead, they place a
     poisoned or 'doctored' article along the path the victim is likely to take,
     but like the female witch they may also poison the food or drink of the
     person they intend to harm.' (Gelfand 1964a : 45). The situation is strictly
     analagous to that of the Cewa where the term *nfiti* is used to refer to both
     witch and sorcerer even though the two modes of attack are distinguished.
     (Marwick 1965 : 79).

4   My analysis here corroborates the hypotheses set forward by J.D.
     MacKnight who notes: 'Women among the Tallensi hold a rather contra-
     dictory position. As mothers they produce children for the descent group
     of which by birth they are not members. It is through them, as outsiders,
     that the lineage continues, yet they are also the foci of segmentation'
     (1967 : 18).

5   See Nadel (1952).

6   During my fieldwork it was always difficult to remain alone for any length
     of time. If I was found alone in my house I was warned that I would begin
     to have evil thoughts about myself and others. I was obliged to devise com-
     plex strategies to achieve solitude.

7   Stories were legion about this kind of *muti* which is the nearest of all to
     simple poison. One old man appeared at beerdrinks with his own personal
     mug and carefully supervised the pouring. It is customary for the beer
     pourer to taste the beer that he distributes lest a subsequent sickness on
     the part of one of the drinkers be interpreted as due to poisoning. In the
     case of food, such is the preoccupation with the possibility of poisoning

that the youngest takes the first handful; if he should fall ill or die his elders will be able to avenge his death!

8   Evans-Pritchard emphasised that Zande 'mystical' explanations did not exclude commonsense explanations. However, explanations in terms of witchcraft involve a forshortening of the chain of events. The Azande 'are selecting the cause that is socially relevant and neglecting the rest . . . In every case witchcraft is the socially relevant cause, since it is the only one which allows intervention and determines social behaviour . . . Since Azande recognize plurality of causes, and it is the social situation that indicates the relevant one, we can understand why the doctrine of witchcraft is not used to explain every failure and misfortune.' (Evans-Pritchard 1937 : 73–4).

9   Most of the *nganga* whom I encountered used the traditional carved wooden tablets, but others employed a variety of innovatory techniques, such as the one who used a small black box containing mirrors. For a detailed description of divining techniques amongst the Shona see Gelfand (1964a).

3. The sociology of spirit-mediumship

1   I discuss this more fully in Introduction.

2   The other well-known exception is measles which is called the sickness of God (*chirwere che Mwari*).

3   There are two words for quite distinct types of lion in ChiZezuru. *Shumba* signifies an ordinary lion while *mhondoro* is the lion form that spirits are supposed to take on while not possessing their hosts. Sometimes the word *mhondoro* is used metaphorically to mean spirit-medium.

4   Many of the wildest confessions which I witnessed could be understood in terms of Levi-Strauss's analysis (1968). Social pressures towards confessions are so strong that the accused are almost visibly manoeuvred into believing and confessing their own guilt. One small girl took many rituals and much dancing before she would fall possessed by the witching spirit which was supposed to be afflicting her. Finally her exasperated mother, who could not afford to spend any more time away from home, told her daughter to fall into trance, 'or else'. Trance followed that night and the girl confessed to various necrophagous practices and gave a detailed description of her familiars.

5   There was almost a one-to-one correlation between the use of black shirts and spirit-mediumship at the time of my fieldwork. This was maybe an everyday way of using the traditional black clothes.

6 . These offices are not strictly ascribed statuses. Genealogical status is a necessary but not sufficient condition for chiefship due to the conflicting succession rules. First born sons, however, are the most likely heirs.

7   For an excellent discussion of this aspect of spirit-mediumship see Garbett (1969).

8   This term is Ioan Lewis's. One of the most exasperating gaps in my data is the statistical information that would be necessary to say more about the epidemiology of spirit-mediumship.

9   The Vapostore (Apostles) are a Zionist sect operating throughout Southern Rhodesia. Their presence in Chiota is not very marked.

10   People of other cultures are often assumed to have the kind of credulity

which would be considered near madness in a close friend or relative. Peter Brown has observed the same occurrence amongst certain historians. 'Faced by so many accounts of the miraculous', he writes, 'the historian of late antiquity usually relieves the strain places on his own credulity by vastly inflating the credulity of his subjects' (Brown 1971 : 96).

11   Zezuru believe that women in childbirth should confess to their extra-marital love affairs lest the birth be difficult or even fatal to mother and child. In this particular case the woman gave birth in an African hospital in Salisbury where the custom is respected by some of the white doctors.

12   Although I visited this medium I never discovered his name. For this reason I shall continue to use *Drum*'s picturesque nickname.

13   The story goes that the medium of *Chaminuka* was captured by Lobengula, the king of the Ndebele, who tried without success to kill him. *Chaminuka* said that he could only be killed by the spear of a sexually immature boy, but that as punishment he would send a plague on the Ndebele; a tribe of people with no knees.

14   This is an accepted belief. Although one medium may act as host for more than one spirit, the reverse is believed impossible.

15   In this book, Gelfand discusses the ritual surrounding Muchatera, the *Chaminuka* medium living near Rusape. There is no reference to any possibility that he might not be the only such medium. I met Muchatera one day while he was sitting outside the DC's office in Marandellas after I had recognised him from the frontispiece of Gelfand's book. When we met, he announced that he was the medium of *Chaminuka*. By way of proof he motioned forward one of his acolytes who was bearing a carefully tended copy of *Shona Ritual*.

16   Gelfand's descriptions (1966) of Shona religion tend to use the term hierarchy as do Abraham's historical researches. Ranger (1967) in his analysis of the Shona Rebellion found that the idea of stable hierarchies did not really explain the situation (see p. 50). The Chiota situation is markedly different from that of the Korekore as described and analysed by Garbett (1966), but this is a subject for another chapter.

17   One of the few analyses of spirit-possession which attempts to understand the possible dynamics obtaining in the spirit world is Robin Horton's essay on Kalabari spirit-possession (1969). He presents the case of a Kalabari medium who began his career as the medium of a 'marginal' water spirit, thus structurally equivalent to David Mudiwa's *nzuzu*. 'This spirit was first announced as the owner of a distant creek, far away from the community's own sphere of interest and operations. Later it came to announce itself as a controller of local waters who acted together with the established big water-spirit Duminea. During a visit by a Shell prospecting party, it assumed responsibility for the oil resources of the neighbouring creeks; and when oil was found, the community gave it credit for the discovery. For some time now, the community has been on the brink of treating it as an object of public cult. With this case in mind, we may look again at some of the myths which tell how village heroes originally came out of the world of the water-people to live with men. I have already offered an intellectualist interpretation of such myths. But it would seem possible to supplement this with a more historical (although highly speculative) interpretation. It is that the heroes, and other big spirits, were originally introduced to the community as minor water-spirits on the heads of *oru kuro* people; and

that they stayed incubating on the sidelines until, at some time of social upheaval and change requiring new interpretative concepts, they came out to make grander claims for themselves' (Horton 1969 : 46–7). Apart from the obvious coincidence that both David Mudiwa and Horton's Kalabari medium both initiated their careers as mediums with water-spirits, the structural similarities between the two cases are significant, for in both situations fluctuations in the spirit world occur in response to change in social relations.

18   Peter Brown has achieved remarkable insights into the sociology of holy men in late antiquity and he makes the very important point that they tend to be over-exposed only in situations of crisis. 'It was through the hard business of living his life for twenty-four hours in the day, through catering for the day-to-day needs of his locality, through allowing his person to be charged with the normal hopes and fears of his fellow men, that the holy man gained the power in society that enabled him to carry off the occasional *coup de theatre*. Dramatic interventions of holy men in the high politics of the Empire were long remembered. But they illustrate the prestige that the holy man had already gained, they do not explain it. They were rather like the cashing of a big cheque on a reputation; and, like all forms of power in late Roman society, this reputation was built up by hard, unobtrusive (and so, for us, partly obscure) work among those who needed constant and unspectacular ministrations' (Brown 1971 : 80–1).

4. Zezuru flexibility and Korekore rigidity

1   The word *ngozi* in ChiKorekore is not to be confused with the same word in ChiZezuru. Among the Korekore *ngozi* is an aggrieved ancestor who expresses his anger by afflicting his descendants. The person who becomes possessed by the *ngozi* spirit does not become the permanent medium of that spirit, which is exorcised as soon as reparation has been effected.

2   Mutota came north, breaking away from the Karanga Empire of the Rozvis.

3   In particular Ranger (1967), Abraham (1966) and Weinrich (1965).

5. Spirit-mediums in ritual action

1   For a person to retain his rights in chiefship he must continue to reside in the chiefdom concerned.

2   Marriages between individuals result in a relationship of perpetual kinship between their two lineages, the wife givers referring to the wife receivers as 'sister's sons' (vazukuru). For a full treatment of this topic, see Garbett (1963a) and Hollemann (1949).

3   After having experienced Anna's cooking, which although excellent was largely vegetarian, I was able to appreciate that attendance at funerals is not simply an emotional act or a social obligation but also a rare chance to eat beef.

4   When a death occurs in a village, no rituals, including marriages, may take place until *kurova guva* has been held. The same prohibitions apply universally during the month of November (*mwedzi yo mbudzi*).

5   Although the ancestors are not believed to inhabit any particular place, it is believed that they are best approached through the pots. In religious

families no journey is undertaken before first kneeling before the pots and asking for protection.

6   Technically the concept of *ngozi* is used to refer to aggrieved ancestor spirits who are believed to plague the living as punishment for some immoral act they or their lineal descendants may have committed. Unavenged murder is the most common cause of *ngozi* affliction. The spirit of the murdered man is believed to plague the lineage of his murderer until they take steps to effect compensation, after which the avenging spirit can usually be laid. In this case the concept of *ngozi* was probably used in a wider non-specific sense, simply as an aggrieved and dangerous spirit for no-one was able to give any specific explanation for it nor to remember a crime on the part of any of the Mutero lineage that might have brought it about.

7   It is not uncommon for white farmers to avail themselves of the rain-making services of Shona spirit-mediums thus furnishing another instance of the retention of such mystical powers as rain-making by dominated autochthons. It will be remembered that the invading Amandebele worshipped at the Karanga shrines in the Matopos hills.

6. Spirit-mediums and missionaries

1   Aberle (1966 : 317) defines transformative movements as social movements which 'aim at a total change in supra-individual systems. The Ghost Dance, millenarian movements and revolutionary movements (by contrast with rebellions) are examples.'

2   This was the so-called 'Mapondera Rising'. Mapondera, the leader, raided the Mazoe area in 1900 and then 'fell back into Korekore country where he allied himself to the chief spirit-medium and ambushed a white patrol' (Ranger 1967 : 358). He was captured by police in 1903 and died seven years later in Salisbury gaol.

3   'Reformative movements', according to Aberle (1966 : 317), 'aim at a partial change in supra-individual systems. The women's suffrage movement, movements in favour of compulsory vaccination, the child labour law movement, and rebellions are all examples.'

4   It can, of course, be argued that the public constitutions of these movements were couched in non-radical terms in order to conceal a more radical stance in reality but this is doubtful.

5   The effects of the implementation of the Native Urban Areas Act of 1947 have been discussed by Gray (1960) who shows that although the Act was designed to bring order out of chaos in the African townships, it in fact brought about a lot of hardship. 'Throughout the Salisbury Municipal area, ... many Africans were finding themselves harshly affected by the Act. Its benefits were not immediately apparent; it involved much disruption; and a storm of discontent with official policy was added to the burden of poverty and the discomforts of the new environment.' (Gray 1960 : 288).

6   The British Government refused to accept the view that the chiefs were, in fact, capable of expressing the opinions of their people, arguing, quite rightly, that as chiefs were paid by the Rhodesian government and depended for their very position as chiefs on government goodwill, they could not be expected to make any public pronouncement against it.

7   In a report in *The Times* of 16 February 1973, headed 'Rhodesia stiffens penalties for aiding guerrillas', was the following comment: 'The Rhodesian government is to get tougher with people aiding guerrillas or failing to report them. Under amendments to the emergency regulations to be gazetted tomorrow the maximum penalty goes up from five to twenty years' imprisonment.' This was no doubt in reaction to a new wave of terrorist incursions into the Centenary area where they had succeeded in establishing some kind of rapport with the local Africans.

8   The *Report of the Commission on Rhodesian Opinion under the chairmanship of the Right Honourable the Lord Pearce* (H.M.S.O. 1972) found that the majority of Africans in Rhodesia were against the proposal that Rhodesia should be granted independence from Britain under a white minority government. Referring to the province of Mashonaland South which includes Chiota Tribal Trust Land, the Report said: 'On the basis of the opinions expressed — both orally and in writing — the vast majority of the Africans rejected the Proposals, whilst an equally big majority of the small European population accepted them' (p. 169).

9   The Ruwadzano was seen by some men as an arena for female politics. They quite seriously believed that the members were really witches using the Methodist Church as a cover.

10 Dip-tanks were a favourite target for attack in other areas as well, largely because they were symbols of the restrictions on cattle holdings which were imposed by the African Land Husbandry Act. Large European farms which lie on the borders of the Chiota Tribal Trust Land were a constant reminder of the injustice of this Act which allowed Europeans to hold large acreages of unused land while obliging the Africans to make do with what they had got by cutting down their herds of cattle and the amount of land under cultivation.

11 These events were barbecues or *braavleis* at which groups of local farmers diverted themselves until late at night with beer and roast beef. Dancing, beer and beef are, of course, the major features of Shona ritual.

12 The legend normally has it that the Chaminuka medium was in fact killed by the Ndebele (see above, p. 43).

13 Linton (1943) pointed out that 'nativistic movements' generally stressed those aspects of traditional culture which were distinctive in relation to the dominant culture.

14 Zezuru culture produces little in the way of carving apart from the famous head-rests which are no longer produced. The dearth of visual art is made up for by the excellence of music.

15 The best account of the structural properties of the chiefs' role in Southern Rhodesia is Holleman's *Chief, Council and Commissioner* (1969).

16 Chief Mangwende sympathised so much with his people's aspirations that he was deposed by the government. Subsequently he became an important member of ZAPU and was put into the Gonakudzingwa restriction camp. The history of his dispute with the government and the District Commissioner of Mrewa is the subject of Holleman (1969).

17 It is interesting to speculate on the importance of the spirit-mediums in precolonial times as spokesmen of popular consensus. Before the setting up of the colonial administration with its policy of indirect rule, chiefs relied for their authority on the support of their followers. It seems likely that the spirit-mediums acted, therefore, as a check on the chiefs' powers.

18 White power in Rhodesia does, in fact, depend on the Africans who are the

NCOs and other ranks in the police and the army. Without their loyalty to their white officers and without the paid services of African informers it would be difficult for the whites, who are outnumbered in the ratio of 10 to 1 by the Africans, to maintain their political dominance.

19 Under the terms of the Witchcraft Suppression Act of 1899 it is an offence to accuse another of using witchcraft. The people of Chiota, especially the *ngangas* and spirit-mediums, are not ignorant of this Act. During my stay with one prominent medium who was well known for his daring in making public accusations of witchcraft and sorcery, a white policeman arrived by Land Rover one Sunday morning. Fear of policemen is strong and universal in Chiota and the many people present were visibly afraid of what might occur. The medium, showing perfect calm, went into trance and dressed himself in his black cloths, animal skins and his black ostrich feather head-dress and walked out to meet the policeman. I was asked to act as interpreter. The medium, in trance, showed the policeman the pile of medicines that he had collected and boasted that by removing the means to do damage to others he was helping the police in their effort to stamp out crime. The policeman was impressed and, after saying that he had always thought that witchcraft and sorcery were purely imaginary concepts but that now he was obliged to believe otherwise, he drove away without further questioning. The incident was followed by all-round hilarity.

20 On one notable occasion it was suggested, during an exorcism, that it would be a good idea to send the witching spirit to a pig, which word had the same connotations as in Western Europe.

21 Crawford (1967 : 141) claims that accusations of witchcraft are more serious than accusations of sorcery, because 'a sorcerer is not inherently evil'. However, as was shown in chapter 3, witchcraft is not a *personal* responsibility. Women who are accused of being witches believe that they are the unfortunate and involuntary accomplices of *shave* spirits which can be exorcised. An accusation of sorcery, on the other hand, is an accusation of predetermined malice.

22 The mediums of Chiota frequently made visits to other Tribal Trust Lands in central Mashonaland and reported the same kind of revival there. They also saw themselves as proselytisers, and the disciple of one medium thought of his master as a latter-day John Wesley. In my frequent visits to the African Townships of Salisbury I encountered much hearsay evidence to support the view that in such areas as Chiweshe, Goromonzi, Mhondoro, Mrewa and Zvimba much the same was occurring as in Chiota. Once I tried to visit a medium in Zvimba but was refused permission by the DC who wrote the following letter:

'I have discussed your proposed visit with the Tribal Authority (Chiefs Zvimba and Chirau) and they both expressed surprise that there could possibly be an important ritual for the induction of a new *svikiro* without their participation or knowledge.

Of recent times there have been attempts by pretenders to conduct ceremonies with the ultimate object of establishing themselves to the detriment of the tribal authority. There is one such charlatan operating in the area at present, and with this knowledge, the chiefs regret that they must decline your request.'

23 A personal communication from Dr Kingsley Garbett.

24 Dr Murphree (1969) claims that in Budya the spirit-mediums did not act as rallying points for nationalist sentiment.

Bibliography

Aberle, D. (1962) 'A note on relative deprivation theory as applied to Millenarian and other cult movements', in Sylvia Thrupp (ed.), *Millenian Dreams
  in Action*, pp. 204–19. The Hague: Mouton.
  (1966) *The Peyote religion among the Navaho*, Viking Fund Publications in
  Anthropology. New York: Wenner-Gren Foundation.
Abraham, D.P. (1959) 'The Monomotapa dynasty'. *Native Affairs Department
  Annual*, no. 36, pp. 59–84.
  (1966) 'The roles of "Chaminuka" and the *mhondoro* cults in Shona political
  history', in E. Stokes and R. Brown (eds.), *The Zambesian Past*, pp. 28–
  46. Manchester: Manchester University Press.
Alpers, E. (1968) 'The Mutapa and Malawi political systems', in T.O. Ranger
  (ed.), *Aspects of Central African History*, pp. 1–28. London: Heinemann.
Beattie, J.H.M. (1961) 'Group aspects of the Nyoro spirit mediumship cult',
  Rhodes Livingstone Journal, no. 30, pp. 11–38.
  (1964) 'The ghost cult in Bunyoro'. *Ethnology*, vol. 3, no. 2, pp. 127–51.
Brown, P. (1971) 'The rise of the Holy Man in late antiquity'. *Journal of Roman
  Studies*, vol. 41, pp. 80–101.
Colson, E. (1969) 'Spirit possession among the Tonga of Zambia', in John Beattie
  and John Middleton (eds.), *Spirit mediumship and society in Africa*, pp.
  69–103. London: Routledge & Kegan Paul.
Crawford, J.R. (1967) *Witchcraft and sorcery in Rhodesia*. London: Oxford Uni-
  versity Press for the International African Institute.
Douglas, M. (1970) *Natural Symbols*. London: Barrie and Rockliffe.
Durkheim, E. (1961) *The elementary forms of the religious life*. New York: Free
  Press.
Evans-Pritchard, E.E. (1937) *Witchcraft, oracles and magic among the Azande*.
  London: Oxford University Press.
Fanon, F. (1967) *The wretched of the earth*. Harmondsworth: Penguin Books.
Firth, R. (1959) 'Problems and assumption in an anthropological study of re-
  ligion'. *Journal of the Royal Anthropological Institute*, vol. 89, pp. 121–
  48.
Fortes, M. (1962) 'Ritual and office', in Max Gluckman (ed.), *Essays on the
  ritual of social relations*, pp. 53–88. Manchester: Manchester University
  Press.
Gann, L.H. (1965) *A history of Southern Rhodesia. Early days to 1934*. London:
  Chatto & Windus.
Garbett, K. (1963a) 'The political system of a Central African Tribe with particular reference to the role of spirit mediums'. Ph.D. thesis, Manchester
  University.
  (1963b) 'The Land Husbandry Act of Southern Rhodesia', in D. Biebuyck
  (ed.), *African Agrarian Systems*. Oxford: International African Institute.
  (1966) 'Religious aspects of political succession among the Valley Korekore

Bibliography

(N. Shona)' in E. Stokes and R. Brown (eds.), *The Zambesian Past*. Manchester: Manchester University Press.

(1969) 'Spirit mediums as mediators in Valley Korekore society', in John Beattie and John Middleton (eds.), *Spirit mediumship and society in Africa*. London: Routledge & Kegan Paul.

Gelfand, M. (1959) *Shona Ritual*. Capetown: Juta.

(1962) *Shona Religion*. Capetown: Juta.

(1964a) *Witch Doctor*. London: Harvill Press.

(1964b) *Medicine and Custom in Africa*. Edinburgh and London: Livingstone.

(1966) *An African's religion*. Capetown: Juta.

(1967) *The African witch*. Edinburgh and London: Livingstone.

Gellner, E. (1969) *Saints of the Atlas*. London: Wiedenfeld & Nicholson.

Gluckman, M. (1950) 'Introduction' to *The Lamba village: Report of a social survey*. Capetown: Communications from the School of Oriental and African Studies.

(1955) *Custom and Conflict in Africa*. Oxford: Blackwell.

(1958) *Analysis of a social situation in Modern Zululand*. Manchester: Published on behalf of the Rhodes-Livingstone Institute by the Manchester University Press.

Gluckman, M., Mitchell, J.C. and Barnes, J.A. (1949) 'The village headman in British Central Africa'. *Africa*, vol. 19, no. 2, pp. 89—106.

Gray, R. (1960) *The two nations*. London: Oxford University Press.

Gulliver, P. (1957) *Labour Migration in a Rural Economy*, East African Studies no. 6. Kampala: East African Institute of Social Research.

Holleman, F. (1949) *Patterns of Hera kinship*, Rhodes Livingstone Papers, no. 17. Manchester: Manchester University Press.

(1952) *Shona customary law*. London: Oxford University Press.

(1953) *Accommodating the spirit amongst some Northeastern Shona tribes*, Rhodes Livingstone Papers, no. 22. Manchester: Manchester University Press.

(1969) *Chief, council and commissioner; some problems of government in Rhodesia*. Assen: Royal VanGorcum.

Horton, R. (1960) 'A definition of religion and its uses'. *JRAI*, XC, 2.

(1962) 'A Kalabari world view: an outline and interpretation', *Africa*, vol. 32, no. 3, pp. 197—220.

(1969) 'Types of spirit possession in Kalabari religion', in John Beattie and John Middleton (eds.), *Spirit mediumship and society in Africa*. London: Routledge & Kegan Paul.

Levi-Strauss, C. (1968) *Structural Anthropology*. London: Allen Lane.

Lewis, I.M. (1966) 'Spirit possession and deprivation cults', *Man(NS)*, vol. 1, pp. 307—29.

(1970) *Ecstatic Religion*. Harmondsworth: Penguin Books.

Linton, R. (1943) 'Nativistic movements', *Am. Anth.*, vol. 32, pp. 230—40.

MacKnight, J.D. (1967) 'Extra-Descent Group Ancestor Cults in African Societies', *Africa*, vol. 37, no. 1, pp. 1—20.

Marwick, M. (1965) *Sorcery in its social setting*. Manchester: Manchester University Press.

Mayer, P. (1963) *Townsmen or tribesmen*. Capetown: Oxford University Press.

Middleton, J. (1960) *Lugbara Religion*. London: Oxford University Press for the International African Institute.

Mitchell, J.C. (1956) *The Kalela Dance*, Rhodes Livingstone Papers, no. 27. Manchester: Manchester University Press.

(1959) 'The causes of labour migration', *Bull Inter-African Labour Inst*. vol. 11, no. 1, pp. 8–47.

(1965) 'The meaning of misfortune for urban Africans', in M. Fortes and G. Dieterlen (eds.), *African Systems of Thought*, pp. 192–203. London: Oxford University Press for the International African Institute.

Murphree, M. (1969) *Christianity and the Shona*, London School of Economics Monographs on Social Anthropology, no. 36. London: The Athlone Press.

Nadel, S.F. (1952) 'Witchcraft in four African societies', *Am.Anth*. vol. 54, pp. 18–29.

(1954) *Nupe Religion*. New York: Glencoe.

Ranger, T.O. (1967) *Revolt in Southern Rhodesia*. London: Heinemann Educational Books.

(1968) 'Connexions between primary resistence movements and modern mass nationalism in East and Central Africa, part 1', *Journal of African History*, vol. 9, no. 4, pp. 437–53, 631–41.

Sartre, J.P. (1967) 'Introduction' to Fanon, F. *The wretched of the earth*. Harmondsworth: Penguin Books.

Shamuyarira, N. (1965) *Crisis in Rhodesia*. London: André Deutsch.

Smith, R.T. (1956) *The negro family in British Guiana*. London: Routledge & Kegan Paul.

Sundkler, B.G.M. (1961) *Bantu Prophets in South Africa*, 2nd edn. London, New York: Oxford University Press for the International African Institute.

Thrupp, S. (1962) *Millenial dreams in action*, Comparative Studies in Sociology and History, Supplement 2. The Hague: Mouton.

Turner, V.W. (1957) *Schism and Continuity in an African Society, a study of Ndembu village life*. Manchester: Manchester University Press for the Rhodes Livingstone Institute.

Van Velsen, J. (1961) 'Labour migration as a positive factor in the continuity of Tonga tribal society', in Aidan Southall (ed.), *Social Change in Modern Africa*, pp. 230–41. London: Oxford University Press.

(1964) *The politics of kinship*. Manchester: Manchester University Press.

(1967) 'Situational analysis and the extended-case method', in Epstein (ed.), *The craft of social anthropology*. London: Tavistock.

Watson, W. (1958) *Tribal cohesion in a money economy*. Manchester: Manchester University Press.

Weber, Max (1946) *From Max Weber: essays in sociology*, translated, edited and with an introduction by H.H. Gerth and C. Wright Mills. New York: Oxford University Press.

(1968) *Max Weber on charisma and institution building*, ed. S.N. Eisenstadt. Chicago: Chicago University Press.

Weinrich, K.H. (Sister Mary Aquina) (1965) 'Modern chiefship and the struggle for power among the Karanga: a comparison of the political process in two Rhodesian reserves'. Ph.D. thesis, Manchester University.

(1967) 'The people of the spirit: an independent Church in Rhodesia', *Africa*, vol. 37, no. 2, pp. 203–19.

Worsley, P. (1968) *The trumpet shall sound*, 2nd edn. London: MacGibbon & Kee.

Bibliography

Rhodesian Government Publications

1951   The African Land Husbandry Act
1957   The African Councils Act
1964   Final Report of the April/May 1962 Census of Africans in Southern Rhodesia. Central Statistical Office, Southern Rhodesia.
1964   The Demand for Independence in Rhodesia. Consultation with the African Tribesmen through their Chiefs and Headmen. The Domboshawa 'Indaba'.

Index

African council, Chiota, 1, 6, 124; income of, 6–7
African Councils Act (1957), 7
African Land Husbandry Act (1955), 6, 8, 124, 130
African National Congress (1957), 109
agriculture, in Chiota, 9, 11
'allergies': believed to herald spirit-mediumship, 30; Thomas's affliction with, 78–80, 103–4
ancestor spirits, 21, 25, 28, 29, 125; competition for favour of, 16; competition for mediumship of, 100; lineages linked to, 28; nationalist movement and, 117, 118; *ngozi* (aggrieved), causing afflictions, 54, 69, 129; seniority among, affects status of medium, 85; spirits attain status of, after *kurova guva* rite, 20, 79; troubles attributed to anger of, 89, and to withdrawal of protection of, 21, 26
Andrew, son of Tatenda, low-level village medium, 68, 69, 100, for father's brother *Mavu*, 71; acting head of village, under Rufu, 70, 84; wife of, 88; employed by James, 91, 102; and *kurova guva* for Rufu, 90, 91, 92; not at Thomas's initiation, 95, 96; villagers of Tatenda side with, 102, 103
Andrew/*Mavu*, 71; consulted by John and Thomas, 80–1, 104; at seance in Ruth's house, 83–4; at seance in own house, denounces Thomas and David/*Kafudzi*, 86–7, 103
Anglican Church, 18, 113, 114
Anna, daughter of Rufu, sister of John, 71, 76; prepares Thomas's special diet, 80, 103; at seance with David/*Kafudzi*, 82, 83
anthropologists, attitude of Africans towards, 1–2
Augustine, son of Rufu, brother of John, 77, 91
Azande: explanations in terms of witchcraft among, 126; traditional faith and scepticism of, towards witch-doctors, 42

Bantu Congress of Southern Rhodesia, 108
beer: brewing of, for *bira* rituals, 31, 90, 93; brewing of, not permissible for Methodist Church members, 113; drinking of, main social activity in winter, 80; ritual drinking of, 9, 21, 26, 31, 32
beliefs, co-existence of two systems of, 105–6
bira (initiation) rituals, 30–2, 94–6, 117
Biri na Ganiri, senior hero spirit of Nyandoro clan, 39, 88
black cloths, worn by mediums at seances, 34, 41, 95, 96, 131
black shirts, worn by mediums, 36, 41
blood: drinking of, in ordeal of new spirit-medium, 32–3, 94
bridewealth, 7, 13, 26; of Carmen, 77, 78, 85, 92, 93; rules for allocation of, 99
British American Tobacco Corporation, 5
British Government: and Domboshawa Indaba, 109; nationalist hopes of action by, 114

Index

British South Africa Company, 11, 107
Budya, Zionist cults among, 122, 132
bureaucracy: appearing in group round David/*Kafudzi*, 47; spirit-mediumship among Korekore as, 56–7, 58, 66
buses, between Chiota and Salisbury, 9
business men, 'medicines' used by, 24–5, 90, 93

Carmen, daughter of Rufu, sister of John, 70, 76; James accused of misappropriating bridewealth of, 77, 78, 85, 92, 93; at seance with David/*Kafudzi*, hostile to John's wife, 82, 83, 100; at initiation of Thomas, 94
case material, in anthropology, 68
cattle: compensation for guilt paid in, 43; killed at rituals, 78, 92, 95, 128; payment for compulsory de-stocking of (1947), 70, 78, 85
cattle-dipping: fees for, 7, 8; nationalist attacks on government officials concerned with, 114, 130
Census, African (1962), 10
Central African Examiner: correspondence in, on Christianity, 111
Chakanyuka, sister's son to Rufu, 92
Chaminuka, hero of the past, 112, 117–18; claimants to be medium of, 43–4; spirit of, 46, 47, 61, 130
Changa, ruler at Zimbabwe, 63
Changamires (successors of Changa), Shona empire of, 62, 63
charismatic leaders, 45–6; as catalysts, transforming individuals into a society, 52; Chiota spirit-mediums as, 4, 45, 46–7, 59, 60; groups based on authority of, 51–2; as materialisation of collective conscience of group, 52; in Zezuru history, 62, 64
Chibwe, mother's brother to Rufu, 91
chiefs, 8–9, 130; on African council, 1, 6, 124; autonomy of, among Zezuru, 64–5; at Dombashawa Indaba, 9, 109, 119; of Korekore, 54; lineages of, 8, 12, 13, 54, 101; and mediums, in Chiota, 119–120, 130; rights of succession to, require residence qualification, 69, 128
Chiota Tribal Trust Land, 2, 5, 6, 16; difficulties of anthropologist in, 1–2; involvement of, with wider polity, 5, 16–17; population of (mid-week), 10; present political and religious trends in, 112–15; religious organisation in, compared with system of Korekore, 4, 57–60, 122
Chiota, Chief, 3, 6
Chipanda, husband of Helen, 77, 82, 83, 90, 91
Chitswachegore, hero spirit, 39, 46, 59–60
Choto, at initiation of Thomas, 94, 95
Christianity: missionaries of, *see* missionaries; period of ascendancy of, opens way to discrediting of spirit-mediums, 61, 108; present African attitude towards, 110–11, 114–15, 122
Christopher, son of Rufu, 78, 83, 92; dance at house of, during *kurova guva* for Rufu, 91; mediumship of, 83, 96, 100; not at Thomas's initiation, 95
clans: dispersed patrilineal of Zezuru, distinguished by totem names, 12; Durkheim on, 51; linked to hero spirits, 19, 28
confessions: during childbirth, 43, 127; at seances, 35, 126
cooking pots: kneeling before, to ask protection from spirits, 81, 128–9
councillors, elected, of African councils, 1, 6, 124
'cow of the mother', given by husband to wife on marriage, 99–100

138

Index

dancing, ritual, 21, 31, 32, 36, 41, 118

David Mudiwa, Methodist preacher, becomes high-level medium, especially for spirit *Kafudzi*, 38–9, 53, 115

David/*Kafudzi*, 34–5, 38–9; analysis of success of, 40–2; charisma of, 46, 47; as detector of witchcraft and sorcery, 39, 121; John consults, 81–3; and Thomas's afflictions and mediumship, 84–6, 104; Andrew's attack on, 86–7; Edward/*Chigara* and, 88–9

Dinka, trance among, 66

District Commissioners, 1, 6, 8, 131

divination, basic function of spirit-mediums, 34; into causes of death, 89; by David/*Kafudzi*, 35, 39, 40; of imminent spirit-mediumship in a person, 30

Domboshawa Indaba (1964), on independence issue, 8–9, 109, 119

Drum magazine, on 'Wild Man' medium, 43–4

drums, at seances, 118

education: missions and increased demand for, in 1930s, 112–13

Edward/*Chigara*, 88; declines invitation from David/*Kafudzi*, 88–9; Thomas comes under patronage of, 88, 89, 93; Thomas in conflict with, 94; at Thomas's initiation, 95

European culture: ancestors and heroes of, 117; exclusion of symbols of, from seances, 119

exogamy, 12, 22, 23

families: nuclear, 7; patrilineal extended, 12

farmers, European: African workers for, 9, 26, 124; barbecues held by, 117, 124; rain-making on behalf of, 97, 129

Filda, sister of John, 82, 83, 94

franchise, in Southern Rhodesia, 5

funerary rites, 20; *see also guva* (first rite), *kurova guva* (second rite), *kudzurura guva* (third rite)

genealogies, showing kinship and spirit-mediumship among people of Tatenda, 72–5

grandfather/grandchild relation, of spirits and men, 31–2

greeting sequences, mediums in, 36

Gumboreshumba/*Kagubi/Murenga*, in Shona Rebellion, 48–50, 61

guva, first funeral rite, 20; for Rufu, 78

head-dresses of black ostrich plumes, worn by mediums, 95, 96, 118, 131

headman: of village, 7, 31; of ward, 6, 124

head-rests, carved (no longer produced), 130

healing: by David/*Kafudzi*, 39; hero-spirits' powers of, 20

Helen, daughter of Rufu, sister of John, 82

Hera, sub-group of Shona: kinship among, 12–13

herbalist/diviners (*nganga*), associated with *shave* spirits, 26, 27, 28; divination of imminent spirit-mediumship by, 30; Mutero as, 69; secret consultations with, in period of decline of mediums, 114

Herbert, son of Rufu, brother of John, 77; at *kurova guva* for Rufu, 91

hero spirits, 4, 19–20, 29; clans linked to, 29; parallel drawn by missionaries

thumb-piano players, 3, 80, 118; in *bira* ritual, 31, 32, 95; may ascribe their
  talents to *shave* spirits, 21; at seances, 39, 41
tobacco, cultivated on large scale in areas bordering on Chiota, 6
totems, Durkheim on, 51
trance, of spirit-mediums, 30, 31, 32, 36
transformative movements, 107, 129
tree, myth of the miraculous, 116
Tribal Trust Lands, 2, 5, 6, 16, 106

Urban Affairs Act (1947), 109, 129

Vapostore sect, 38, 126
Vatsunga lineage of hero spirits, linked to Nyandoro clan, 84, 88
Veronica, younger sister of Thomas's mother, 70, 94
village sections, 7, 12
villages, 7–8; core lineages of, 4, 12; low-level spirit-mediums in politics of, 48

Waddilove (Nenguo) Methodist Mission (from 1892), 16, 76, 112
wards (territorial units), 7, 8; core lineages of, 12
'Wild Man', claimant to mediumship for *Chaminuka* spirit, 43–4
witchcraft, 18, 22–3, 125; accusations of, 16, 100, 131; detection of, by David/
  Kafudzi, 39, 121; distinguished from sorcery, 22; divining power of a medium
  may be thought of as affected by, 34; new preoccupation with, 121, 122; as
  source of disunity, 121; withdrawal of protection of ancestor spirits opens
  way for, 21
Witchcraft Suppression Act (1899), 131
witching spirits, 22; exorcism of, 22, 39, 121, 131; matrilineal inheritance of
  possession by, 22, 28
women: in Chiota family and business affairs, 11, 124; clubs of, in Methodist
  Church, 113, 130; excluded from hereditary office, 37; as mediums, 37–8; as
  outsiders, 22, 38, 125; as points of division within patrilineage, 15–16, 99

Zande, divination among, 35–6
Zezuru, 6; dispersed exogamous clans of, 12; history and religious organisation
  of, 62, 64–7; involvement of, in political struggles, 16; magico-religious
  beliefs and organisation of, compared with Korekore system, 4, 57–60
Zhava, medium at initiation of Thomas, 95
Zimbabwe, ruling and religious centre, 62, 63, 64
Zimbabwe African National Union (ZANU), 4, 19; banned (1964), 16, 109; in
  conflict with PCC, 1, 109, 114, 120
Zimbabwe African People's Union (ZAPU), 109, 130
Zionist cults, in central Mashonaland, 122
Zwimba Reserve, 38